DATE DUE

BRODART   Cat. No. 23-221

THE STORY OF
CANADIAN
WHISKY

THE STORY OF
CANADIAN
WHISKY

LORRAINE BROWN

Fitzhenry & Whiteside

200 Years of Tradition: The Story of Canadian Whisky

Fitzhenry & Whiteside
195 Allstate Parkway
Markham, Ontario
L3R 4T8

Editing: Margaret Hoogeveen
Design: Arne Roosman
Graphics: New Concept PrePress

Printed and Bound in Canada by McLaren Morris & Todd Ltd.

Canadian Cataloguing in Publication Data

Brown, Lorraine
    Two hundred years of tradition : the story of Canadian whisky

Includes index.
ISBN 1-55041-094-6

1. Whiskey — Canada — History.   2. Whiskey industry — Canada — History.   I. Title.

HD9395.C3B76 1994   641.2'52'0971   C94-930864-1

The Seagram Company Ltd.

1430 PEEL STREET, MONTREAL, QUEBEC, CANADA H3A 1S9

CO-CHAIRMAN

Dear Reader:

This book, which covers the 200-year history of Canada's whisky industry, is long overdue. The role that Canadian whisky played in the building of our nation has largely been overlooked by Canadian historians and teachers. Few people realize, for example, that the grist mills of Upper Canada (as Ontario was called at that time) were also the country's first Canadian whisky distilleries, or that Canadian whisky played a very important role in the lives of the pioneers, not only as a beverage, but also as currency in the early days.

Every nation should be aware of its past. By knowing the past, we gain a better understanding of ourselves. We may even gain some insight into the future. It was with these thoughts in mind that the Seagram Museum was opened 10 years ago in Waterloo, Ontario, a museum devoted to spirits and wine.

As part of its tenth anniversary celebrations, The Seagram Museum commissioned this book, <u>200 Years of Tradition: The Story of Canadian Whisky</u>. This fascinating book and the exhibit on the same subject that will travel from coast to coast in Canada will fill a gap in Canada's history. It is my hope that you will find this book both educational and enjoyable.

Sincerely,

Charles R. Bronfman

Acknowledgements

The author would like to thank the following people who read and commented on the manuscript: Gale Bost, Anne Chafe, Art Dawe, David Hyde, Norman J. McDonald, Karen Mingay, Guy Paquet, Doug Rubbra, Laura Scott, and Dick Tyssen.

Sandra Lowman, librarian/archivist at The Seagram Museum, helped with the photo research. Phil Dietrich, designer at The Seagram Museum, kindly photographed materials from the museum's archives.

Artifacts from The Seagram Museum

x.   Act of Parliament, ARC 82.1.10
xi.   Seagram's V.O. jug, 82.73.1
2.   Tavern sign, 94.3.1
4.   Jug, 89.3.1
12.   Domestic copper pot still, 84.35.10
12.   Field barrel, 82.19.38
16.   Gooderham and Worts rye whisky, B93.1.1
21.   Spirit safe, 82.12.5
40.   Seagram whiskies (bottom picture), left, B82.10.5; middle, B94.3.3; right, B82.6.8
56.   Mash sampler, 82.2.16
56.   Yeast container, 82.49.85
64.   Poster, 83.32.1
74.   Ontario government dispensaries price list, ARC 82.3.11
80.   Gooderham and Worts rye whisky, B84.0.108
93.   Canned whisky: Knickerbocker, B94.3.2; Chickencock B94.3.1
97.   Pedigree bourbon, B89.6.1
100.   Illustration, ARC 93.3.12
104.   V.O. advertisement, 94.E1.4
105.   Labels, 94.E1.5
134.   Barrel, 82.87.1

Table of Contents

A Day in Upper Canada, 1830

It's a late fall day in the Bathurst District of Upper Canada. Farmers throughout the district have harvested their crops of barley, wheat, oats, and rye, and have been delivering it to Edward Bellamy's mill, in the Bathurst District, to be ground into flour and animal feed.

Some of the farmers have travelled several kilometres to the mill and are camped there for a few days while their grain is ground. Tired after the autumn harvest, they enjoy a few days' rest and the companionship of their fellow settlers. A crock of whisky makes the rounds. Talk revolves around crops, the weather, politics, and life in the New World.

The harvest was plentiful this year, and Bellamy has ground thousands of bushels of grain. For his milling services, he charges the farmers one-tenth of their crops, and the payments have been piling up. What is Bellamy to do with all this grain? Storage facilities are limited, besides which, stored grain would rot or be eaten by rodents. Delivering the bulky grain to far-off markets would be unwise considering the condition of the primitive roads and the bounty of grain everywhere.

Bellamy's solution — one adopted at many of Upper Canada's small water-powered grist mills — is to turn the excess grain into whisky. One bushel of grain yields roughly three gallons. The spirits can be stored indefinitely and profitably transported to markets some distance away.

In fact, distilling the grain has been so profitable that Edward Bellamy has invested in a new still this year. Delivered recently from Scotland, the gleaming 100-gallon copper pot still has the greatest capacity of any still in the Bathurst District. Bellamy produces his whisky in a shed adjoining the mill, and proudly invites the farmers to come in and see his new acquisition. Inside the shed, grain mash ferments in a large wooden tank and a wood fire crackles in a stone oven under the 100-gallon still. Whisky, crystal clear and steaming hot, drips slowly from the coiled condensing worm into an oak barrel. Its sweet scent wafts over the still autumn air.

Bellamy's mill and distillery represent the origins of a major Canadian industry and a unique, new product: Canadian whisky. Growing beyond its humble beginnings in the grist mills of Upper Canada, Canadian whisky will soon be in demand all over North America and Great Britain. And, although Bellamy couldn't have known it, the Canadian whisky industry will one day provide the major source of revenue by which his country will achieve nationhood.

Farmers taking their crops to the mill

AN ACT

TO LAY AND COLLECT A DUTY UPON STILLS.

WHEREAS, for the better support of the Government of this Province, it is expedient to increase the Revenues thereof; We Your Majesty's most dutiful and Loyal Subjects, the Representatives of the People of the Province of Upper Canada, in Assembly met, do most humbly beseech Your Majesty that it may be enacted, and be it enacted by the King's most excellent Majesty, by and with the advice and consent of the Legislative Council and Assembly of the Province of Upper Canada, constituted and assembled by virtue of and under the authority of an Act passed in the Parliament of Great Britain, intituled, " An Act to repeal " certain parts of an Act passed in the fourteenth year of His Majesty's Reign, in- " tituled, " An Act for making more effectual provision for the Government of " the Province of Quebec, in North America, and to make further provision for " the Government of the said Province," and by the authority of the same, That from and after the fifth day of April next, there shall be raised, levied, collected and paid yearly, and every year, unto His Majesty, His Heirs and Successors, to and for the use of this Province, and towards the support of the Civil Government thereof, of and from all persons having and using a Still or Stills, or hereafter to have and use a Still or Stills, for the purpose of Distilling Spirituous Liquors for sale, a sum not exceeding one shilling and three-pence, lawful money of this Province, for every gallon which the body of such Still or Stills shall or may be capable of containing, in manner herein after mentioned.

Preamble.

Duty to be paid for every gallon which a still, in use, is capable of containing.

II. And whereas it is expedient to make provision for the service of the current year, Be it enacted by the authority aforesaid, That the said Duties shall begin and be payable for the seven months, which will elapse between the fifth day of September, and the fifth day of April next ensuing the passing of this Act, to be paid at and after the rate of seven-pence half-penny, lawful money as aforesaid, per gallon, in manner herein after mentioned.

Provision for the current year, to determine in April.

III. And in order that the size of the several Stills to be employed for the purposes aforesaid, may be more truly ascertained, and the Duties to be imposed thereon more easily collected, Be it enacted by the authority aforesaid, That from and after the fifth day of November next, it shall not be lawful for any person to make use of any Still or Stills, for Distilling Spirituous Liquors for sale, until he shall have obtained a Licence for that purpose; and every person desirous of obtaining such a Licence, shall, in a written requisition for the same, to be made in manner hereafter mentioned, specify and set forth the number of gallons which the body of the Still or Stills he proposes to use, does or do contain, which specification shall be inserted in the Licence to him to be granted; And in case any person shall make use of any Still for the purpose of Distilling Spirits for sale, without having obtained such Licence, or shall make use of any Still or Stills for the purpose of Distilling Spirits, of larger dimensions than that or those specified in his Licence or requisition, or shall have in his possession any Still or Stills erected or set up over a Furnace or Fire-place, so as the same may be used for Distilling, capable of containing singly or together a greater number of gallons in the body or bodies thereof, than the number of gallons specified and set forth in his Licence

Method of ascertaining the contents of rateable stills.

Penalty for using or having in a situation to be used, stills of larger dimensions than specified in the licence.

In 1794, the British government established Canada's first still tax, thereby creating the country's main source of revenue for the next fifty years. (From The Seagram Museum Collection)

INTRODUCTION
Canadian Whisky: 200 Years of Tradition

The year 1994 marks an important milestone for Canada's whisky industry. It was in 1794 that the first tax on stills was issued in this country. For the next two hundred years, Canadians made and drank whisky while the government collected an ever-increasing share of the revenue.

Canada's whisky industry was born in the grist mills of Upper Canada (Ontario). Small, local distilleries proliferated at mills throughout the province and, to a lesser extent, in Lower Canada (Quebec). By 1840, two hundred such small enterprises had been licensed. Eventually these distilleries were replaced by a few very large enterprises: Hiram Walker, Seagram, Corby, and Wiser. These companies, established in the 1850s, along with Gooderham and Worts, which preceded them by twenty years, have created a roughly defined whisky region for Canada, in southern Ontario.

The custom of making a distilled beverage from grain has traditionally been limited to those of Gaelic ancestry. The first people to make whisky were the Irish, in the thirteenth century. The Scots followed with their famous spirit in the late fifteenth century. When Irish and Scottish settlers came to the United States and Canada, they brought their distilling traditions with them, adapting their recipes to the crops and conditions of the New World.

Bourbon, the "straight" corn whisky developed by American distillers in the eighteenth century, was the world's third whisky. Americans had been turning their crops of corn and rye into whisky for about one hundred years when the United States broke ties with Britain in 1776. Many of the United Empire Loyalists who fled north to Canada at that time became grist mill operators. These new Canadians had a major influence on their adopted country's distilling customs.

The American influences, combined with those of Irish and Scottish settlers who came directly to Canada from the Old World, resulted in the development of the world's fourth great whisky: Canadian whisky, a unique blend of spirits made from corn, rye, and barley and aged at least three years in charred oak barrels. It has a flavour and lightness all its own.

Whisky is one of the unsung traditions of Canada's pioneers. This book will give that tradition some much deserved recognition by documenting the

Seagram's V.O. crock. (From The Seagram Museum Collection)

making and drinking of whisky through two hundred years of Canadian history. It follows the Canadian spirit from the grist mill to the corporate boardroom of 1994. It analyses whisky's role in the development of the Temperance Movement, and the tumultuous, lawless Prohibition Era in Canada and the United States. It outlines the evolution of whisky-making technology in Canada, bringing the reader from the simple pot stills of the miller-distiller to the massive, computer-operated plants that make Canadian whisky now. It presents the innovative marketing that accompanied whisky's rise from a bulk agricultural product sold for twenty cents a gallon to a high quality beverage drunk in the most exclusive nineteenth-century men's clubs. It looks, finally, at the decline in the industry today and the growing problem of smuggling and illicit alcohol production as consumers try to find ways to avoid high taxes.

Through it all, Canada's great distilling companies have continued to produce and market their fine whisky. Ownership in some cases has passed on to new interests: multinational corporations with headquarters in other countries. But the names and the whiskies of Hiram Walker, Joseph E. Seagram, and the others live on today — a tribute to the high quality of the products conceived by their founders a century and a half ago.

Canadian whisky is better known outside Canada's borders than within. It is especially well known in the United States, whose citizens consume 86 per cent of Canada's whisky production. With this book, the Canadian whisky industry invites Canada to look back at this unsung chapter in her history, and to celebrate a great Canadian product.

The fermenting room at Hiram Walker & Sons, Windsor, Ontario

CHAPTER 1

Old Customs in the New World

Drinking in Pioneer Canada

From the late 1700s until about 1830, the citizens of both Canada and the United States appear to have been decidedly intemperate. Although drinking was probably heavier in the United States, Canadians were regular tipplers, too. With 147 distilleries and 96 breweries serving a population of 500 000 in Upper Canada in 1842, someone was obviously drinking.

A bulk agricultural product made at the local mill, whisky cost only about twenty to thirty cents a gallon and was always in demand. In fact, it was the main beverage of the pioneers, especially in Upper Canada. Farmers took a crock or small barrel with them to the fields. For factory workers, a "coffee break" was a shot of rum or whisky at 11 a.m. and 4 p.m. — provided by the employer, of course. Children were sent off to school in the morning fortified — and warmed, presumably — by a "nutritious" glass of whisky. Whisky appears to have been as ubiquitous as diet colas are today. And unlike modern Canadians, who monitor their drinking carefully for health reasons, nineteenth-century Canadians believed that alcohol had important medicinal qualities. So

important, in fact, that non-drinkers were considered a bad risk as far as health insurance was concerned.

As the districts of Upper Canada were settled, inns were often the first public buildings to go up, and they soon became the focal points of pioneer life. Political meetings, voting, sales of crown land, court sessions, even church services went on at the inn until such time as court houses, churches, and town halls could be built. Since virtually every inn had a licence to sell alcohol, drinking accompanied many of these events. At a penny a glass, everyone could afford it.

Bellamy's mill in the Bathurst District (now Eastern Ontario), had a hundred-gallon still in 1832. The mill building is now part of Upper Canada Village, a living history museum near Morrisburg, Ontario.

With new areas of settlement opening up, many people travelled by stagecoach. The roads were poor, so travellers could only expect to cover a few miles each day. Taverns and inns were quite common along the roads. Between Hamilton and York (now Toronto, Ontario), for example, a distance of sixty kilometres, twenty taverns lined the road in 1833. Yonge Street, running north from York to Lake Simcoe, had even more. Coaches stopped frequently for refreshment, and the drivers were given free drinks in exchange for bringing in their clients. No one worried about drinking and driving.

Nowhere was drinking more in evidence than at pioneer working bees. Catharine Parr Traill, a writer and naturalist who immigrated to Canada from England in 1832, describes the bee that built her first home in the backwoods near Peterborough, Ontario:

> Sixteen of our neighbours cheerfully obeyed our summons; and though the day was far from favourable, so faithfully did our hive perform their tasks, that by night the outer walls were raised. The work went merrily on with the help of plenty of Canadian nectar (whiskey), the honey that our bees are solaced with.[1]

In Sydenham Township, north of Owen Sound, Ontario, the village of Leith was home to one of the many small distilleries that dotted the

An early tavern sign. Whisky was readily available in pioneer times, and quite inexpensive. (From The Seagram Museum Collection)

countryside. A history of the township describes how the "Water o' Leith" was an indispensable requirement at barn raisings:

> The whiskey manufactured at Leith sold for 40¢ to 60¢ a gallon at both Leith and Owen Sound. It was in great demand at barn raisings where a pailful was placed on a piece of squared timber and every one could drink at his pleasure. Apparently there were very few who ever got drunk at these raisings. The farmer who refused to furnish whiskey for a raising was known as a tightwad.[2]

"Few who ever got drunk"? Social historian Graeme Decarie might question that remark. His research showed that brawling, serious injury, and even death were common at bees.

Parties, working bees, inns, and taverns weren't the only places where our ancestors enjoyed a social drink. Even during a routine trip to the general store, the ever-present whisky could be found. In the town of Orono, Ontario, writes a local historian from that area, "a barrel of whisky usually stood in every store, with a dish beside the tap, and

Saskatchewan men and women raise their glasses in a pioneer toast, ca. 1880s.

customers just helped themselves."[3] Besides the inexpensive local whisky, well-off customers would also be able to purchase imported whisky from Scotland and Ireland. No grocery store would have been complete without this essential item.

By all accounts, alcohol appears to have played a fairly central role in the lives of the pioneers. But what else were they to drink? There were no soft drinks or fruit juices, and tea and coffee were not available in the earliest days of settlement, with the exception of some herbal teas. The lack of refrigeration meant milk soured quickly — in any case, it was deemed a children's drink. Many Europeans who had come from big cities were not in the habit of drinking water, because in their experience water was not usually potable. And it would be decades before North America had the vineyards to produce grape wine. Wine was imported from Europe, but only the rich could afford it. The remaining choices were beer, cider, rum, cordials, and whisky.

Given the difficulties of life in a new country and the loneliness and homesickness many settlers must have felt, it's not surprising that they would have taken solace in a drink or two. Historians who specialize in the social history of alcohol have found that in frontier conditions, especially in countries with an agricultural resource base such as Canada, the United States, or Australia, people drink heavily — especially

when liquor is widely and easily available, and cheap.

While whisky was the main beverage of Upper Canada, the situation differed in other parts of the country. Rum had always been most favoured in the Atlantic provinces, as it was along the eastern seaboard of the United States. The availability of sugar, molasses, and rum itself, delivered by ships running from the Caribbean to the eastern seaboard, created an early custom of rum drinking in this part of North America. Even today, statistics show that much more rum is consumed per capita in the Atlantic provinces than in the rest of Canada.

Lower Canada was also a whisky-making province in the early days of the industry, but much of the production was shipped to Europe. People here did drink whisky, but not as much as their neighbours did in Upper Canada. Lower Canada had a strong tradition of beer drinking, established from the time when Intendant Jean Talon set up the

Three gentlemen pose for a portrait at the Retlaw Hotel in Enchant, Alberta, 1914.

3

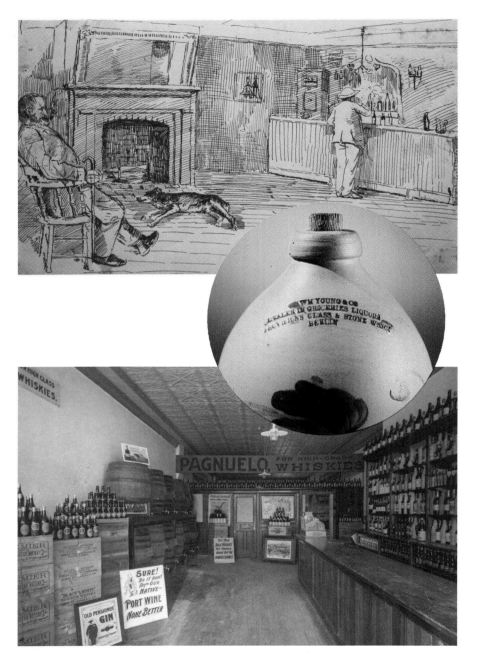

The Red Lion Hotel, Bloor Street, York, ca. 1888

Grocery stores carried liquor as well as food in the days before the Temperance Movement. Crocks like this were the first "returnable bottles." (From The Seagram Museum Collection)

Pagnuelo's liquor store in Calgary, Alberta, 1912. Note the spigots in the barrels, from which customers would have filled their own crocks with Pagnuelo's "bulk whiskies."

province's first brewery in 1668. Talon encouraged the people to drink beer rather than spirits. Canada's first still was established in Quebec City in 1769 to produce rum from imported molasses. But it was gin that became the favoured spirit in Quebec, after Dutch gin maker Jan Melcher established a gin distillery in Berthierville in the 1870s. Even today, statistics still show a strong preference for the Dutch, Geneva-style gin in Quebec.

Whisky was popular in the Prairie provinces during the early days of settlement. It came into the region from two sources: the Hudson's Bay Company, which created new markets for its imported Scotch whisky as the area was settled, and the notorious American whisky peddlers, who set up palisaded forts where they traded furs for bad whisky with the Native People. One of the most notorious of these was

A whisky-bottling operation in the basement of the Hudson's Bay store, Winnipeg, 1905. The Hudson's Bay Company imported Scotch in bulk and bottled it under their own brand names. The Corby barrel in this picture indicates that they also bottled Canadian whisky.

Fort Whoop-Up, near present-day Lethbridge, Alberta. The Dominion government created the North-West Mounted Police — which later became the Royal Canadian Mounted Police — to clean up the uncontrolled liquor traffic in western Canada. Colonel Sam Steele, who led the first detachment of mounted police into the northwest, described the trade that went on at Fort Whoop-Up:

> The trader stood at the wicket, a tubful of whisky beside him, and when an Indian pushed in a buffalo robe to him through the hole in the wall he handed out a tin cupful of the poisonous decoction. A quart of the stuff bought a fine pony.[4]

While the Canadian Pacific Railway was being built, the North-West Mounted Police were again called in to maintain law and order among the thousands of workers and to stem the flow of liquor into the region. The labourers had little else on which to spend their money, and smugglers developed all kinds of schemes for delivering their goods: eggs were emptied of their contents and the shells filled with liquor; tins of peas and corn held liquor rather than vegetables; and sometimes "bibles" sold in the work camps turned out to be tin containers of whisky.

Canada's alcohol consumption records begin in 1871, so one can only speculate about how much people were drinking before that by analysing anecdotal reports and

Fort Whoop-Up, near present-day Lethbridge, Alberta, was one of the most notorious of the whisky-trading posts. Here American whisky traders gave Native People whisky in exchange for buffalo skins.

Calgary House, Calgary's first hotel, was built in 1883, when the Canadian Pacific Railway was under construction in Alberta.

indirect evidence. The number of distilleries, liquor shops, and taverns in operation for a given population provides the best source of insight into the subject. In 1836, the Bathurst District of Upper Canada (the area around Smith Falls and Perth, west of Ottawa), with a population of thirty thousand, supported six distilleries — probably producing an average of about fifty gallons of whisky a day — thirty-five shops that sold liquor, and sixty-five inns. Toronto had a tavern for every 137 citizens, including men, women, and children. Port Hope, a town of 2500 in the 1850s, had eight distilleries. From these figures, it would seem that, in Upper Canada, drinking was quite popular.

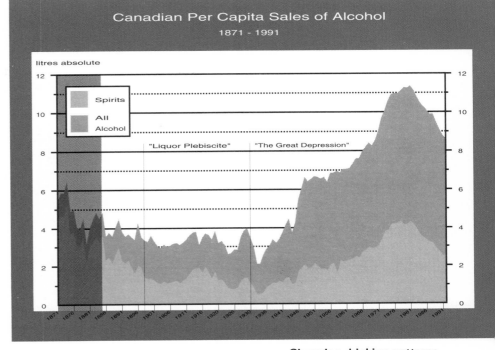

Canadian Per Capita Sales of Alcohol
1871 - 1991

Changing drinking patterns in Canada, 1871 to 1991. The highlighted portion of the graph shows that spirits (mainly whisky) played a far more prominent role in Canadians' drinking habits in the past than they do today.

200 Canada's First

Whisky

Given the origins of Upper Canada's settlers, it would have been unusual if they had *not* established stills as one of their first items of business in the New World. Indeed, they didn't waste much time in taking care of this essential requirement. By 1827 — twelve years after the first settlers arrived to clear the land and establish farms in the Bathurst District — the government had already licensed two dozen stills in the small villages of the area.

Whisky had played an important role in the daily lives of the Irish and Scots for several centuries. The Irish

had invented whisky in the thirteenth century, and gave it the name *uisgebeatha*, meaning "water of life." The word *whisky* comes from this old Gaelic word. When they settled in the New World, the Irish and Scots brought their ancient whisky-making traditions with them. In their experience, malt (germinated barley) was the raw material of whisky. But in Canada, the homeland traditions had to be modified. Without the time and resources to set up malt houses where grain could be dried slowly over wood or peat fires, Canada's first distillers improvised with what-

ever was at hand: oats, rye, wheat, corn, even peas and potatoes.

The United Empire Loyalists also brought innovations to Canada's pioneer whisky industry. During the century before Upper Canada was settled, American colonists had been developing new distilling techniques unique to the New World. Bourbon, the best-known American whisky, originated in Bourbon County, Kentucky, and has corn as its principal ingredient. In Upper Canada, over many years, the customs of the American Loyalists and the Scottish and Irish settlers mingled, setting the stage for the development of a uniquely Canadian whisky made from corn, barley, and rye.

What was that early whisky like? One can only speculate, though English traveller John McTaggart gives us some inkling of its quality. Writing during his three-year sojourn in Canada in 1829, McTaggart described the pioneer whisky he came across as being "made of frosty potatoes, hemlock, pumpkins and black mouldy rye."[5]

Mouldy rye? The millers probably saved the best of the crop for milling into flour, leaving the poorer quality grain, sweepings, and middlings to go into the still (middlings being coarse particles of all sorts of grains left over from the flour milling process). Nor did that early whisky benefit from any mellowing contact with oak. It went straight from the still into the barrels, crocks, and kegs of the pioneers, unaged and clear in colour. Second distillation and ageing were refinements that would come later.

The potency of pioneer whisky has been the subject of speculation. It is quite certain that the early Canadian whisky, which was the product of a single distillation in a pot still, was similar in strength to the distillate that today comes from the first pot still

(the wash still) in the distillation of Scotch malt whisky. The alcoholic strength of the distillate is approximately 20 per cent. This would make the early Canadian whisky much weaker than the Canadian whisky available today, which is 40 per cent alcohol by volume, and, as historian Merrill Denison wrote, more like fortified wine than whisky.

In those early days, people were probably less concerned with the quality of whisky than with its effects. Reflecting on pioneer tastes in his 1924 publication, *The Windmill and Its Times*, E.B. Shuttle-

worth wrote the following good-natured remarks:

People bought their whiskey very much as they now purchase their wine. If it pleased the palate and possessed that titillating quality in the mouth, which is the precursor of a genial glow which shall presently pervade the whole system, they cared little for its ... [alcohol content measurement], but were content with the less scientific but vastly more interesting organoleptic test.[6]

During the construction of the Canadian Pacific Railway, a seventy-kilometre wide "railway belt" was established as a liquor-free zone, to maintain law and order among the construction crews.

A frontier saloon in Donald, British Columbia, 1884–85.

Bar in Boissevain, Manitoba, 1912. The framed poster on the left is a 1906 lithograph featuring the King's and Queen's Plate winners from the Joseph E. Seagram stables.

Saloon in the Northwest
Territories, ca. 1885. Note the
barrels with spigots in front,
and the labelled bottle —
probably Scotch imported by
the Hudson's Bay Company.

This circular exhorted parish priests in Quebec to approve as few tavern licences as possible, and only for individuals of known integrity.

Lettre Circulaire à Messieurs les Curés de Campagne.

MONSIEUR,

POUR entrer dans les vûes du Gouvernement qui a sagement fait annoncer dans la Gazette de Québec du 15 du présent mois, qu'après le 5 Avril prochain nul n'obtiendra le licence pour vendre des liqueurs dans les paroisses de campagne, sans s'être auparavant muni de l'attestation du Curé du lieu et du Capitaine de Milice; nous vous exhortons à faire usage de cette marque de confiance d'une manière qui réponde aux intentions qu'a le Gouvernement de maintenir partout l'ordre, la paix et les bonnes mœurs.

Vous observerez donc de ne donner cette recommendation qu'au plus petit nombre que vous pourrez, et seulement à des personnes d'une probité reconnue, chez qui vous ayez lieu d'espérer qu'il ne se passera aucun désordre occasionné par l'usage immodéré des boissons.

Je suis bien parfaitement,

MONSIEUR,

Votre très-humble et très-obéissant Serviteur,

✝ JEAN FRANCs Ev. d'Almire, Coadjr. de Québec.

QUEBEC, 16 Mars, 1787.

BON POUR COPIE.

Plessis

3.

A nineteenth-century Montreal street scene. Painted by James Duncan.

Did Canada
"Drink Herself to Nationhood"?

"From the quantity of grain produced for which a market cannot readily be found, the inhabitants have been induced in many places to set up stills."[7] These words flowed from the feather pen of John Graves Simcoe, the first lieutenant-governor of Upper Canada, in 1794.

Simcoe's report was not lost on his superiors back in England. The distilleries of Scotland and Ireland had become an important source of government revenue in Great Britain just six years earlier, when King George III levied Britain's first still taxes in 1788. The British wasted no time in setting up a similar tax system in their North American colony. Canada's first still tax, established in

John Graves Simcoe (above), lieutenant-governor of Upper Canada from 1791 to 1796, issued Canada's first still licence in 1794.

1794, required distillers to pay one shilling and three pence (about twenty-five cents) annually for each gallon of still capacity. Mr. Bellamy, whose mill in the Bathurst District is now part of Upper Canada Village in Morrisburg, Ontario, would have paid about twenty-five dollars each year for the privilege of running his still. He probably hung his licence from a nail on the wall in his small distillery.

By 1801, when the population of Upper Canada was less than fifteen thousand, fifty-one still licences had been issued. Each new licence meant more revenue for the growing colony's coffers. In fact, taxes on distilled beverages were the main source of government revenue in those days, prompting one historian to remark that Canada "had to drink herself to nationhood."[8] In 1840, after the union of Upper and Lower Canada, the government imposed the first excise or gallonage tax on Canadian spirits — two pence per gallon — and increased the still tax to forty pounds annually per still. By this time there were two hundred licensed distilleries producing whisky in Upper and Lower Canada, most of them associated with grist mills. District inspectors were appointed to collect the taxes. With Confederation in 1867, taxes on distilled beverages were doubled, from thirty to sixty cents a gallon. (Canada had also changed over to the decimal system of currency in the intervening years.) In 1874, the tax rose to seventy-four cents a gallon. Canada's distillers

have been making enormous and increasing contributions to Canadian government revenues ever since.

Canadian distillers were more compliant about the taxes than their colleagues south of the border. Farmer-distillers in western Pennsylvania saw the new still tax and excise tax levied by the American government in 1791 as an affront to their freedom. In the American Whiskey Rebellion that took place between 1791 and 1794, several federal excise agents were tarred and feathered before the situation was finally defused.

Some of Canada's early settlers brought small, domestic copper stills with them to the New World. But the 1794 still tax made it illegal for anyone to operate stills with less than ten-gallon capacity. This eliminated most domestic and small-scale stills. (From The Seagram Museum Collection)

Farmers took whisky into the fields with them in pioneer times. They may have used a portable field barrel like this one. (From The Seagram Museum Collection)

200 YEARS OF TRADITION
THE STORY OF CANADIAN WHISKY

At the same time that dozens of small-scale distillers were turning out whisky in the nation's grist mills, two major distilleries were being established in Toronto and Montreal. On the shores of Lake Ontario in Toronto, beside its landmark windmill, Gooderham and Worts established Upper Canada's first major distillery in 1837. It was to become Canada's longest-running distillery.

Molson's

Canadian ... Whisky?

The credit for Canada's first large-scale distillery goes to Montreal and the illustrious Molson family. As every Canadian knows, the Molson name today is synonymous with beer. If it hadn't been for increased excise taxes and the growth of the Temperance Movement in the mid-1800s, the Molson name might have been appearing on our whisky bottles today, too.

Brewing beer was the main enterprise John Molson embarked on after immigrating to Montreal from England in 1782. But along with the

John Molson (1763–1836) was Canada's first industrial-scale distiller. His Montreal distillery, established in 1799, produced 250 000 gallons of whisky per year, making it the largest in the country.

brewery he established in 1799, Molson also built a distillery that produced 250 000 gallons of whisky annually. John Molson's son Thomas, who was born in 1791 and who became the family's most knowledgable distiller, also purchased breweries and distilleries in Kingston and Port Hope (both in Upper Canada) in the early years of the nineteenth century. With a capacity of 910.5 gallons, the Kingston still may have been the largest in Upper Canada. The total still capacity for the province in 1833 was 5138 gallons.

The Molsons are an anomaly in the story of Canadian whisky for three reasons. First, they operated for only forty years, abandoning distilling in favour of beer, even though the former seemed to have a promising future. Second, of all the early distillers, the Molsons were the only ones that did not begin as a flour-milling enterprise that switched to whisky production. And third, they operated in Lower Canada, not Upper Canada, where the industry was born. The Molsons dominated the Canadian distilling industry from 1820 to 1867, and no history of the whisky industry in Canada would be complete without them.

John Molson and his son Thomas made important contributions to the advancement of the art and science of distilling. Both of them took a scientific approach to the subject, experimenting extensively with production methods and keeping detailed notes of their work. The

This 1859 agreement between John H.R. Molson, son of Thomas, and Hiram C. Sherman, a New York distiller, indicates the Molson family's interest in learning the latest distilling techniques.

Molson papers contain evidence that the father and son were interested in incorporating the latest distilling technologies from New York and Scotland. There is, for example, correspondence between John J.R. Molson (Thomas's son) and a New York distiller, indicating that the former had trained in the art and science of distilling in New York. Also among the papers are sketches of Scottish distilleries drawn by Thomas Molson. Anxious to learn about the latest developments taking place as a result of the Industrial Revolution in Great Britain, Thomas travelled to Glasgow, Scotland, in 1815 and to New York and England in 1836. The purpose of these trips was to visit distilleries, purchase new equipment, and learn distillation techniques.

The Molsons were responsible for another landmark event in distilling in Canada: in 1821 they sent the first shipment of Canadian whisky to England. The shipment — probably high-proof whisky to be used in blending — marked the beginning of a major Canadian export industry.

The English had never really been whisky drinkers like the Irish and Scots. England's upper class had tended to drink wine and brandy from France, while the working class drank ale and gin. But times were changing. The Napoleonic Wars (1792 to 1814) cut off supplies of French wine and brandy. As a result,

Montreal's harbour must have looked something like this when the Molsons were shipping whisky to Europe. The photograph was taken by William Notman, 1885.

Coins minted by Molson's bank

15

the English upper class developed a taste for whisky, especially blended whisky. Scottish and Irish distillers tried to meet the demands of this growing new market, but it proved to be beyond the capacity of their distilleries. Canada — mainly the Molsons — happily filled the gap. Thanks to Napoleon, Canadian pine provided spars for the British navy ships and, for a few decades, Canadian whisky filled the decanters in the best English households. But the export market was not to last. By 1846, Scottish distillers had expanded enough to provide for the British market.

By the 1860s, the Molson family had shifted its focus towards brewing rather than distilling, in spite of Thomas Molson, who foresaw a healthy future in whisky. There were

About 1880, distillers began bottling their whisky. This bottle of Gooderham and Worts rye whisky is dated 1884. (From The Seagram Museum Collection)

several reasons for the decision. First, the export market had dried up. Second, government was increasing taxes on distilled beverages. The third reason was the rise in temperance agitation. Beer was considered an acceptable drink by temperance proponents in the early days of the movement, while whisky was not. The Molson distillery in Montreal finally closed in 1867. But from 1820 until that time, the Molson family had thoroughly dominated the Canadian distilling scene.

Gooderham and Worts: Upper Canada's Oldest Distillery

While the Molsons made whisky in Montreal, William Gooderham and his brother-in-law James Worts were busy establishing the first major distilling enterprise in Upper Canada. Gooderham and Worts opened their grist mill in York (Toronto) in 1832.

James Worts came to Canada in 1831, establishing the grist mill at the mouth of the Don River. The Worts family came from the east coast of England, where windmills provided the main source of energy, so a windmill must have seemed like a natural choice to power the waterfront enterprise. On April 20, 1832, the steamer *Great Britain* arrived at York carrying the main shaft for the windmill, while a schooner delivered the millstones and other parts to a wharf at the foot of Church Street.

William Gooderham (1790–1881)

The Gooderham and Worts windmill became an important Toronto landmark. The tower, six stories high, dominated the waterfront for many years, and the company became known as "The Windmill." Eventually the windmill was destroyed by a storm, but even before that happened it had been replaced by steam power. There simply wasn't enough wind on Lake Ontario's shore to run a windmill to power a grist mill.

William Gooderham, a miller from Suffolk, England, followed his brother-in-law James Worts to Canada in 1832 with about fifty-four people, including members of the two families, servants, and eleven orphans. Gooderham invested the three thousand pounds he had brought with him in Worts's milling business, and thus the partnership of Worts and Gooderham was born. James Worts died in 1834, before the distillery was even established, and the firm changed its name to "William Gooderham, Company." In 1845 Worts's son, James Gooderham Worts, who had come to Canada with his father as a boy, moved into his father's position as partner with William Gooderham. That year, the firm's name was changed to "Gooderham and Worts."

"Distillery Commencing 3rd Nov. 1837." These words, heading a record book for the still house, unequivocally mark the beginning of the distilling enterprise. The distillery was housed in a wooden building adjacent to the grist mill. The still was a wooden column still with a capacity estimated to be about five hundred gallons. (A description of the technology used in the early Gooderham and Worts distillery can be found in chapter 4.) The first run of whisky was made from 36 bushels

James Gooderham Worts (1818–1882)

The Gooderham and Worts distillery on the Toronto waterfront, 1896. Illustration by A.H. Hider.

of wheat, 304 bushels of middlings, and 27 bushels of malt probably produced at the mill. The first product of the new still was sold to a store-keeper on nearby King Street.

In the 1830s, the growing town of York, with its many taverns and grocery stores selling liquor, had distilleries at Castle Frank, York Mills, and

The Gooderham and Worts distillery in 1918

The engine room at Gooderham and Worts. (From the *Canadian Illustrated News*, 1863)
In 1994 the City of Toronto approved a plan to restore the Gooderham and Worts complex, converting it into a modern neighbourhood of condominiums, offices, restaurants, shops, and parks.

This photograph, taken at Gooderham and Worts in 1916, indicates that the stillman may have sat and waited for the whisky to begin flowing into the tail box.

Todmorden Mills, to name just a few. Eventually, probably because of increasing taxes, these smaller distilleries closed. But Gooderham and Worts, with its markets in Upper Canada for "common" whisky (aged for only two to twelve months) and in Lower Canada for its higher quality, aged Toddy and Old Rye, as well as its overseas markets, continued to thrive.

In 1840, Gooderham extended his trade to Montreal and then beyond Canada. He also added rectifying equipment, which allowed the distillery to produce the high-proof spirits needed for medicine and industrial alcohols. The original mill and distillery were replaced in 1861 with a much larger, five-storey distillery complete with storehouses, elevators, and a private wharf on the waterfront. The new distillery employed 150 men and produced 2 1/2 million gallons of whisky a year, making it the largest in Canada. Gooderham and Worts had overtaken Molsons, who by the 1860s were focussing their efforts on brewing and banking.

The city of Toronto was obviously proud of the new Gooderham and Worts facility. The *Toronto Globe*, in its *Annual Review of the Trade of Toronto* for 1861, called the new plant, "the most important contribution to the manufacturing interests of Toronto.... It is the largest in Canada, and in point of completeness and general arrangement, is equalled by few on the continent." The *Canadian Illustrated News* devoted its supplement of April 25, 1863, to the new plant and its whisky-making technology. In 1877, the *Montreal Gazette* described Gooderham and Worts as one of the most important companies in Canada. Their final paragraph indicates

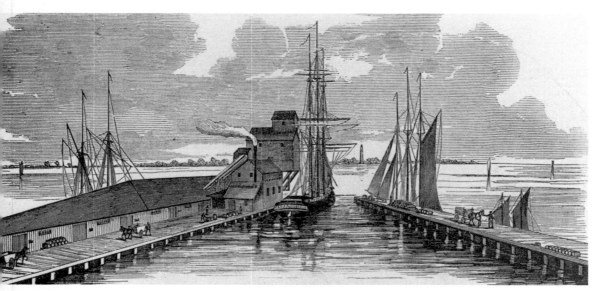

Gooderham and Worts's storehouse, wharf, and grain elevator

the significance of the Gooderham and Worts empire at that time:

> To sum up their business briefly — they have the largest distillery in the world; they feed more cattle, directly and indirectly, than are fed by any one establishment outside Texas; they run a railway to the great benefit of Toronto and the northern country; and they own a bank which there is none in this country ranking higher in public confidence.[9]

By 1875, Gooderham and Worts were producing one-third of all the spirits in Canada, paying over $1.5 million in taxes to the Dominion government and shipping large quantities of whisky to England, the United States, and South America. In terms of fixed capital, number of employees, added value, and value of products, the Gooderham and Worts distillery ranked fourth among Ontario businesses. William Gooderham was one of Toronto's most prominent businessmen; he was also president of the Bank of Toronto, in which Worts was the second-largest stockholder. The Gooderham and Worts empire also included lake transportation, railways, retailing, and woollen mills.

In 1902, Gooderham and Worts reached its maximum production level, at two million gallons of spirits. That year, they set up a new company, General Distilleries Limited, to produce industrial spirits. It was a fortuitous move: in 1916 all Canadian distilleries were converted to the production of industrial alcohol for the war effort. That year, General Distilleries entered into a contract with the Imperial Munitions Board. British Acetones Toronto Limited was set up to produce acetone from corn. Canada produced 78 per cent of the acetone required by the Allies during World War One, and 75 per cent of it came from British Acetones Toronto Limited.

Harry Hatch, an entrepreneur from Deseronto, Ontario, who had worked as sales manager for the Corby distillery near Belleville, bought Gooderham and Worts in 1923. Though no longer in the hands of the original families, the company still holds the honour of being Canada's longest continuously running distillery.

During World War One, Gooderham and Worts created a new company, British Acetones Toronto Limited, to produce acetone for the war effort.

The Arrival of the Excise Officer

With the establishment of large distilleries in Canada, excise officers were assigned to individual distilleries. The government created a special class of excise officers for this purpose in 1873 — officers qualified as "men of undoubted good character for their honesty and sobriety." The excise officer's task was to protect the revenue from the manufacture of spirits by supervising the entire distilling process. This meant that no operation could be carried out in a distillery without the presence of an excise officer. As time went by, distillers came to recognize the excise staff as being almost as integral to the whisky-making process as the distiller himself. Distilleries created offices for these government employees and collaborated with them in every way. Many officers were assigned to each large distillery. For example, the Seagram distillery in Waterloo kept twenty officers busy.

However, as of 1986, the position of resident excise officer in distilleries does not exist. Today, the officers use a post-operational audit approach, looking for fluctuations in production and auditing distilleries' books. They also help new distilleries set up their books, approve labels, sign age and origin certificates, and monitor the sealing of trucks filled with whisky. The role of excise officer is no longer the exclusive domain of men. Canada hired its first female excise officer in 1981.

John Davis, an early Canadian excise officer, 1868. Excise officers were assigned to all of the country's distilleries. Note the instrument on top of the barrel for removing the stopper or bung; the "thief," which was used to remove samples from the barrel; the brass hydrometer in a glass tube on the table; and a record book.

The locked spirit safe, where the whisky flowed from the still, was the domain of the excise officer. He alone held the keys, and the distillery could not operate unless an excise officer was present. (From The Seagram Museum Collection)

CHAPTER 3
The Golden Age of Canadian Whisky: 1850 to 1920

In the 1850s, dozens of small distilleries throughout Upper Canada succumbed to drastically changing circumstances. Improvements in distilling technology left the small-scale operators behind. The increased taxes levied by the government, especially high after Upper and Lower Canada united in 1840, made distilling unprofitable for small operators. A growing network of railroads eliminated the necessity of making whisky near the place of sale. Finally there were the social changes taking place in Canadian society. Cities grew while the population in rural areas shrank.

But there must have been something in the air in Upper Canada during the 1850s, something telling enterprising young men that the time was ripe for Canada to develop a large-scale distilling industry. Between 1857 and 1859, four men were to join Gooderham and Worts in Upper Canada in establishing distilling operations that would eventually turn southern Ontario into Canada's premier whisky-producing region.

J.P. Wiser and Hiram Walker came north from the United States, both of them seeing great potential for milling and distilling enterprises across the border. Joseph E. Seagram was born in Canada of English parents. Henry Corby emigrated from England. All four started in the flour-milling business, and all four soon abandoned the milling side of their operations to focus on a more lucrative product in the markets of the day: whisky. Towns sprang up

THE WORLDS' GREATEST SHIPMENT OF RYE WHISKY

THE "CORBY SPECIAL" WHISKY TRAIN. CARRYING A RECORD SHIPMENT OF RYE WHISKY

NEARLY HALF A MILE OF CARS, containing over 50,000 GALLONS of Corby's Famous Rye Whisky, equivalent to 300,000 QUART BOTTLES.
To get the best Rye Whisky, insist on getting CORBY'S SPECIAL SELECTED."

An endless train filled with Corby whisky

around their distilleries. Two of them — Corbyville and Walkerville — were named for the distilleries and their founders.

These four men, with their talent for business and their eye for opportunity, probably recognized several factors that gave Canada West (Ontario's name between 1840 and 1867) great business potential in the 1850s. First, the growing network of railroads and shipping routes ensured reliable transportation to distant markets. The Grand Trunk Railway of Canada was incorporated in 1852 to build rail lines from Toronto to Montreal. This company established routes throughout Ontario and hooked up with the U.S. rail system as well.

To young entrepreneurs, distilling would have looked particularly promising as a business venture. On the one hand, small distilleries were closing as the country grew beyond its rural, agrarian beginnings, so the competition was shrinking. On the other hand, the population was growing quickly, creating markets that justified large-scale distilling. Canada's population grew from 2 436 297 people in 1851 to 3 229 633 in 1861.

The growing Temperance Movement in the United States also made Canada, with its laxer laws, look

J.P. Wiser aimed for perfection in both his distillery and his farm operation. Rysdyk, pictured at centre, was Wiser's most beloved racehorse.

attractive to American entrepreneurs, as did the country's wide-open spaces and high-quality, inexpensive farmland. Another important factor was the American Civil War (1861 to 1865), which reduced stocks of food and beverages in the United States and created new export opportunities for Canadian distillers. The time was ripe: southern Ontario was on the threshold of becoming Canada's whisky region. All that was required was some energetic, hardworking individuals with the vision to get the wheels in motion.

 ## J.P. Wiser

John Philip Wiser, the son of a Dutch farmer from New York State, had the required ambition. Born in 1825 in Trenton, Oneida County, "J.P.," as he was known, developed an early interest in livestock. As a young man, he made a name for himself buying and selling cattle and supplying markets throughout New York State. J.P. went into business with the Ogdensburg, New York, firm of Averell and Egert, and later became a partner in the company. Averell owned a distillery in Ogdensburg and had purchased another in Prescott, Canada West. In 1857, J.P. moved north to manage the Prescott operation. With his interest in cattle, he saw the distillery not only as a way to produce whisky but, perhaps more importantly, as a means of fattening cattle.

Prescott was looking for entre-

John Philip Wiser (1825–1911)

preneurs like J.P. An 1859 county directory attempted to lure businesses to the growing town on the banks of the St. Lawrence with this description: "One of the best sites for Trade and Commerce in the Province — united with Ottawa by direct Railway — also with Montreal, Toronto, and Kingston by the Grand Trunk Railway, a port of call for all Canadian steamers and traders east and west."[10] An important transportation centre, Prescott moved goods that had come down the St. Lawrence River westward throughout the province. It seemed a suitable choice for a distillery location.

At that time in the eastern Ontario counties of Leeds and Grenville, where Prescott is located, five distilleries were all competing to become the biggest whisky producer in the two counties. Production increased from around seventy thousand gallons to over eighty-four thousand gallons per year at the Averell distillery after the hard-working and energetic young Wiser took over; the competition soon fell behind. Five years after moving to Prescott, J.P. bought out his partner. The *Conservative Messenger*, Prescott's newspaper of the day, announced, "J.P. Wiser, successor to C.P. Egert and Co., superior quality liquors. Also corn, cornmeal and oatmeal for sale."[11]

Fires were a major problem for Canada's early distilleries — an inevitable result of the lethal combination of wooden buildings, air filled with flour dust, and the constant fires necessary for keeping the stills in operation. After fire swept through

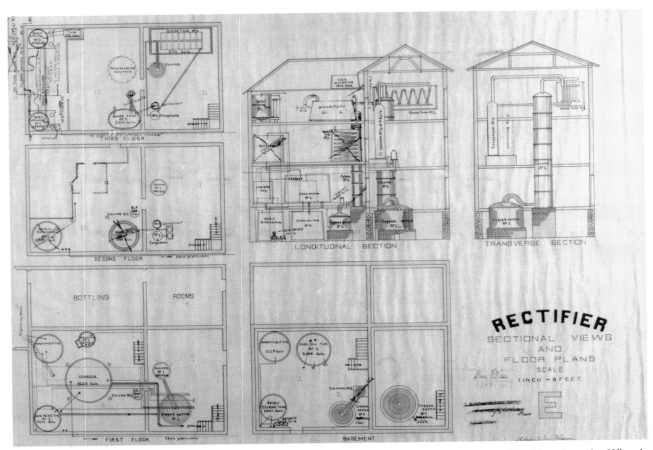

Rectifier plans for Wiser's distillery

the Wiser distillery in 1864, Wiser rebuilt it on a larger scale, incorporating the new distilling technology developing rapidly in both Great Britain and New York.

The new distillery paid government revenues of about two thousand dollars daily and supported sixty families. New cattle barns housed two thousand head of cattle, most of them destined for export to the United States and Great Britain. The size of Wiser's agricultural operations is staggering: in one record year he purchased a total of thirty-seven thousand cattle and sheep. In 1875 the first shipment of steers travelled from a Canadian port to Europe. They were Wiser animals fattened on Wiser distillery wastes, and they were the start of an agricultural export industry that became one of the most important for Canada. Distillers' wastes, rich in protein and carbohydrates, actually hold more food value than the original corn, because the dried grains recovered after distillation contain protein-rich yeast. Cattle fattened on distillers wastes were well known for the tenderness and flavour of their meat.

Wiser was a perfectionist in all his undertakings. He hired the best cabinet makers and coopers for the distillery. The wood panelling in his Prescott mansion was a work of art, created by a craftsman who had worked on the panelling in the Parliament Buildings in Ottawa. His Clydesdale horses and Durham and Hereford cattle were his pride and joy. His farm operation was considered a model by the Ontario Agricultural Commission. He also maintained huge stock farms in Kansas and Texas. Like some of his distilling colleagues, notably Joseph E. Seagram, J.P. Wiser was a lover of thoroughbred racehorses and bred them in his stables. His beloved racehorse, Rysdyck, purchased in New York for ten thousand dollars, was one of the finest racehorses on the continent.

Wiser was also a perfectionist when it came to making whisky. He continually upgraded the distillery equipment, and spent much time in the rectifier room, working to improve his product. Many poor-quality and adulterated whiskies proliferated in those days, and the demand for a pure, high-quality product drove Wiser, the perfectionist,

Rushton Hall, Wiser's mansion in Prescott

The master craftsman who carved the rich panelling inside the Wiser mansion also worked on the panelling in the Parliamentary Library in Ottawa.

to produce it. He maintained a consistent standard for Wiser's Red Letter Rye and Wiser's Canada Whisky, and earned a reputation for producing a reliable, high-quality product. No one is certain when, where, or by whom the term "Canadian Whisky" was first used. Wiser may have been the first, when he exhibited his products at the Chicago World Fair in 1893.

Wiser also took an active interest in political affairs, both in his community and beyond. He spent eleven years on the Prescott Town Council and served as a Liberal member of Parliament for one session beginning in 1878. During his time in Parliament, he travelled to western Canada to advise the government on the suitability of the land for ranching.

About 1885 the Wiser distillery reached its pinnacle. J.P. must have been proud of his empire on the St. Lawrence at that time. Looking down from his plush Victorian office, he could watch as his employees unloaded tonnes of coal and thousands of bushels of wheat, barley, corn, and rye at the docks. His whisky, with its reputation for high quality and purity, sold throughout the United States, Canada, China, and the Phillipines. His distillery, now employing over one hundred, was the third largest in Canada.

J.P. died in 1911. His two sons took over the company, but neither had the business ability of their father. In 1932, J.P. Wiser's distillery was purchased by Corby.

**Joseph Emm Seagram
(1841–1919)**

Joseph Emm Seagram

Octavius Augustus Seagram and his wife, Amelia Stiles, immigrated to Canada from Wiltshire, England, in 1837. They purchased two farms and a tavern in Fisher Mills, near Galt (now Cambridge, Ontario). The couple had two sons, Joseph Emm, born in 1841, and Edward Frowde. The two boys were orphaned in their teens. They lived for the next six years at a boarding school for boys in Galt.

After spending a year at business college in Buffalo, New York, Joseph Seagram returned to Canada, where he worked as a bookkeeper and manager at various mills in Galt and Stratford. In 1864, William Hespeler hired Joseph to take care of his interests at the Granite Mills and Waterloo Distillery in Waterloo while Hespeler

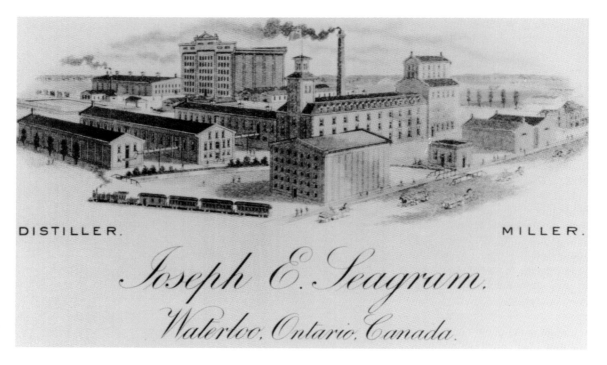

DISTILLER.   MILLER.

Joseph E. Seagram.

Waterloo, Ontario, Canada.

Joseph E. Seagram's distillery, ca. 1880

travelled in Europe. Along with a business partner, George Randall, Hespeler had established a mill, distillery, and dry goods store in 1857. Like many mill operators of the time, the partners distilled their surplus grain into whisky. When Seagram was hired, the Granite Mills and Waterloo Distillery was producing fifty thousand gallons of spirits each year and had fifteen employees.

Seagram saw great potential for the distillery side of the business. Over the next few years he bought into

the company and then proceeded to buy out his partners. In 1883 he changed the company name to "The Joseph Seagram Flour Mill and Distillery Company." He eventually sold the dry goods store to focus his attention on whisky production.

At this time, in Canada, whisky was made with a variety of combinations of grains, but it was all "straight" whisky, not blended as in the new approach to whisky making adopted in Scotland and Ireland. Seagram was among the first Canadian distillers to blend whiskies. In 1883 he created a new blend, and named it "Seagram's '83" to celebrate his takeover of the business.

The distillery had begun exporting whisky to the United States and Europe in 1875. Seagram greatly expanded the export side, especially to the United States, where his products gained popularity for their smooth, light quality. By the 1890s, large quantities of Seagram's '83 were making their way to New York, Chicago, and Detroit. The Seagram name soon became well established in the United States, and for many years Seagram whisky was the most popular Canadian whisky in the U.S. market.

Seagram incorporated the company in 1911, changing the name to "Joseph E. Seagram and Sons, Limited." His sons, Edward and Thomas, began to take an active role in the company. That year, the company released another new brand, Seagram's V.O., to celebrate the marriage of Thomas Seagram. The story goes that the idea for the blend that makes up V.O. was developed during an after-dinner conversation with his sons. V.O. probably stands for "very own," as this was a whisky blend that Seagram created for his own family.

While his business was whisky, Seagram's passion was horse racing. Now a wealthy man, Seagram advanced horse racing in Canada, establishing it as a popular hobby among the wealthy elite. He imported high-quality breeding stock from the United States and Britain. Horses from the Seagram stables were Queen's Plate winners for eight consecutive years, beginning with Seagram's horse, Terror Colt, in 1891. Seagram's stables achieved fifteen plate wins in all. The *Canadian Magazine* described Seagram as, "the greatest Canadian horse breeder."

Like Wiser, Seagram was active in politics. He was a Conservative member of Parliament for Waterloo North during the Liberal years of Sir Wilfrid Laurier. He participated in a variety of local organizations, becoming an influential and respected member of the community. His black and gold racing colours were adopted by the city of Waterloo and later by the University of Waterloo.

Joseph Seagram died in 1919. He had built his Waterloo distillery into a major exporting company and his

Seagram's distillery and flour mill, 1890

brand names were widely known and respected. It was the Seagram name, with its reputation for excellence, that stirred the interest of Samuel and Harry Bronfman. In 1928, Joseph Seagram's sons sold the distillery to the Bronfmans, who amalgamated it with their company, Distillers Corporation Limited. In the next few years, the Bronfmans were to turn the Seagram company into the largest producer of spirits in the world.

This 1939 label was released in time for the King and Queen's visit to Canada in that year. The illustration, done by A.H. Hider in 1906, shows some of the King's and Queen's Plate winners from the Seagram stables.

200 Hiram Walker

Hiram Walker was born in 1816 in Douglas, Massachusetts. He was only nine when his father died, and at the age of twenty he left Douglas to start life on his own. Walker moved to Boston, where he worked in a dry goods store. But the West beckoned. After two years, in 1838, he moved to Detroit, then a town of nine thousand people.

By 1846, Hiram Walker had saved enough money to go into business on his own as a grocer and liquor dealer. New prohibitory laws made it illegal for grocers to sell liquor, however, so Walker focussed on food instead. He began making vinegar, an important commodity in the days before refrigeration, and before long Walker vinegar was widely sought after for its consistent, high quality. Walker also worked as a grain merchant, supplying millers in the Detroit area with wheat.

Perhaps the combination of making vinegar and dealing in grain gave Hiram Walker the idea of becoming a distiller. His work as a grain merchant had brought him into Canada West, and Walker could see great business potential in the British colony. He was attracted by Canada's inexpensive land and labour, its plentiful corn and rye crops, and its good rail transport. The Great Western Railway had been completed from Niagara Falls to Windsor in 1854, completing transportation links to Montreal, Portland, and New York. Furthermore, Walker saw little competition in the flour-milling and distilling business in southwestern Ontario. Canada also represented an escape from the Temperance Movement, which at that time was far stronger in the United States than in Canada.

Hiram Walker began by purchasing land in Upper Canada in 1856 and opening his new steam-powered flour mill and distillery in 1858, calling it "The Windsor Distillery and Flouring Mill." He produced whisky according to demand, and the demand grew quickly. Walker continued as a grain merchant in Detroit, but before long the distillery demanded his full attention. In 1859 he and his family moved to Windsor, Ontario, and took up residence in "The Cottage," a frame house west of the mill. After five years, though, the Walkers moved back to Detroit and Hiram commuted by ferry and coach each day — a round trip of three hours.

Walker's whisky and flour were in great demand, and the company grew to include malthouses, a cooperage, a copper shop, a planing mill, a lumber yard, a brick yard, and a dairy farm. As the number of employees grew, Walker began to build a town for them. In 1870 he commissioned the community's first church. A public school was housed in the basement of the church, until Walker replaced it later with a brick

Hiram Walker (1816–1899) (above) in 1855, three years before he founded his distillery

schoolhouse. Utilities were provided free of charge. In 1869 the government opened a post office and officially recognized the town's name as ''Walkerville.'' A company fire brigade was established; Walker built a fire hall and reading room, which doubled as a social club for the community. By 1882, Walkerville had a population of six hundred, most of whom were Walker employees.

Today Hiram Walker would be called a workaholic. He never stopped working. Besides the distillery and farm operation, he was also involved in several furniture and lumber companies and in real estate. He also got involved in the rapidly expanding railway business. In 1885, Walker incorporated the Lake Erie, Essex and Detroit River Railway. By 1901 the line ran all the way to St. Thomas, becoming an important element of the area's economic activity. Lumber, fresh fish, vegetables, and fruit went by rail from Essex County to the United States. Walker established a ferry service between Walkerville and Detroit as well. In his later years, to encourage him to take it easy, his sons bought him two pleasure boats and the family acquired Ile aux Peches in the St. Clair River for a summer home. But

In 1929, Hiram Walker & Sons received a royal warrant from the British royal family. The warrant entitled the company to use the royal arms in connection with their business.

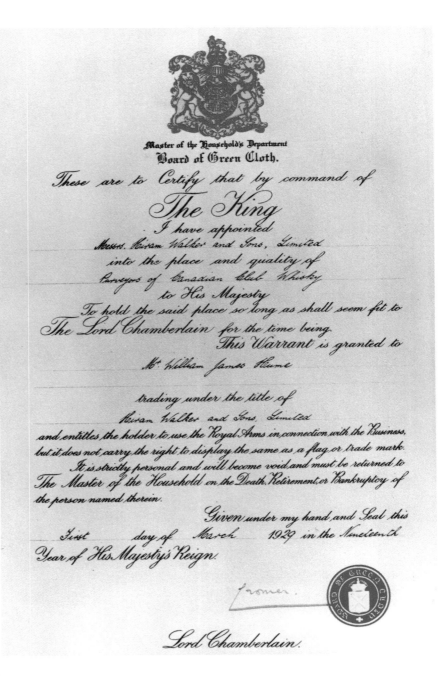

Master of the Household's Department
Board of Green Cloth.

These are to Certify that by command of

The King

I have appointed
Messrs. Hiram Walker and Sons, Limited
into the place and quality of
Purveyors of Canadian Club Whisky
to His Majesty

To hold the said place so long as shall seem fit to
The Lord Chamberlain for the time being.
This Warrant is granted to
Mr William James Hume

trading under the title of
Hiram Walker and Sons, Limited
and entitles the holder to use the Royal Arms in connection with the Business, but it does not carry the right to display the same as a flag or trade mark.
It is strictly personal and will become void and must be returned to The Master of the Household on the Death, Retirement, or Bankruptcy of the person named therein.

Given under my hand and Seal this
First day of March 1929 in the Nineteenth Year of His Majesty's Reign.

Cromer.

Lord Chamberlain.

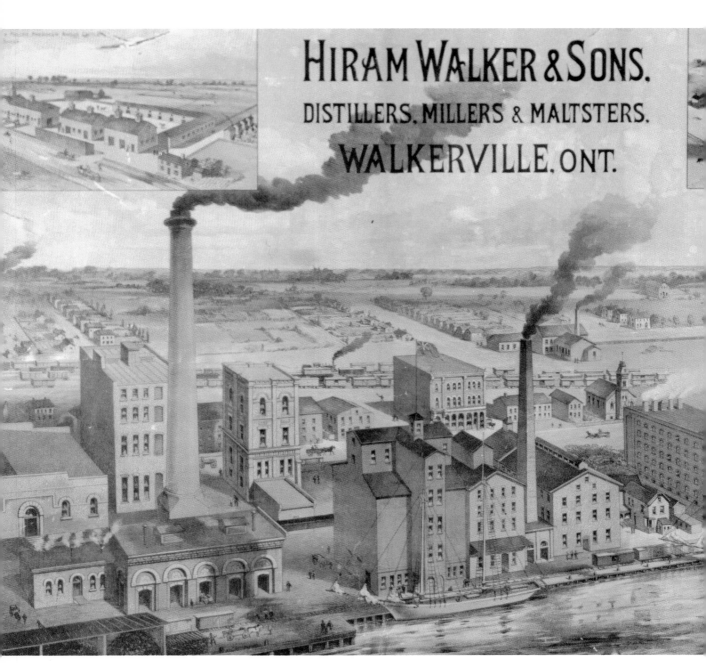

HIRAM WALKER & SONS.

DISTILLERS, MILLERS & MALTSTERS.

WALKERVILLE, ONT.

The Hiram Walker mill and distillery were established at Walkerville (now part of Windsor, Ontario) in 1858.

even in his old age, Hiram continued to work hard.

In spite of his accomplishments in other areas, it was in distilling that Hiram Walker was to leave his most important legacy. Walker was responsible for a number of important precedents in the Canadian whisky industry. He was the first to use multi-column distillation. His patent for this achievement can be found in the archives at the Walker head office in Walkerville. He may have been the first to create the blended product known today as Canadian whisky. Exactly where and when Canadian whisky was first made remains a matter for speculation, but some experts feel that the honour should go to Walker's Club whisky. Walker was also the first to heat the barrel warehouses so that the whisky matured for twelve months of the year. He was among the first to give brand names to his products and to put it into labelled bottles. He may also have hired the first travelling salesmen of spirits.

Walker employees in front of the Walkerville Smoking and Recreation Hall, 1923. The hall was just one of the facilities that Hiram Walker provided for his employees.

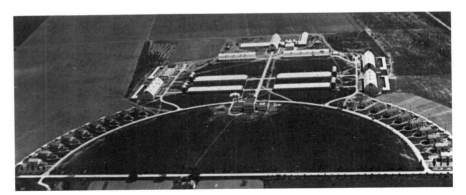

Aerial view of Walkerside Dairy Farm, 1920, with workers' houses in the foreground

33

The main office building at Hiram Walker — a magnificent renaissance structure of red sandstone, built in 1894

Hiram Walker continued to run his empire, which included railroads and real estate, until he was well on in years.

birthday, the people of Essex County paid tribute to the man who had done so much for them, by presenting him with a magnificent bronze statue. Made by Tiffany & Co. of New York, the bronze represents three soldiers on horseback. The presentation speech provides insight into the relationship Walker had developed with his employees:

> The people of Walkerville, therefore, point with pride to the fact that they have been for years in the enjoyment, through the thoughtfulness of your firm, of advantages and comforts which are rare under similar conditions of private control, and it is doubtful whether there could be found anywhere a more happy relationship between capital and labour, or a greater average of comfort among all classes than has existed here.[12]

Walker was also the first North American whisky producer to receive the royal warrant from the British royal family. Walker received this great honour for Canadian Club in 1898; thereafter, he proudly displayed the royal coat of arms on the label. Canadian Club continued to receive this honour from the House of Windsor until 1979.

In 1890, Walkerville became an incorporated town. On July 4 of that year, Hiram Walker's seventy-fourth

The bottling department at Hiram Walker & Sons Limited

34

Hiram Walker died in 1899 at the age of eighty-three. Under the direction of his three sons, Edward Chandler, James Harrington, and Franklin Hiram, the company continued to prosper. By 1910, sales of Hiram Walker's whisky were second only to Seagram among distillers in Canada. In 1926, with the violence of the Prohibition Era burgeoning around them, Hiram's grandsons, Harrington E. Walker and Hiram H. Walker, sold the company to a consortium of businessmen led by entrepreneur Harry Hatch.

200 Henry Corby

Henry Corby arrived in Canada from England in 1832 to settle in the small lumbering community of Belleville, Upper Canada. He had apprenticed as a baker in England but was otherwise totally unprepared for the remarkable future he eventually built for himself as the head of a major distilling company. Legend has it that Henry had only one sovereign in his pocket when he arrived with his wife and family in Belleville. He started a small bakery, and in just six years was the leading baker in the town.

Soon after, tragedy befell the young Corby family. His wife and three children drowned when their sleigh went through the ice on the Bay of Quinte. Henry later married his first wife's sister, and the couple had twelve children.

After playing a role in the 1837

Henry Corby (1806–1881)

Rebellion, Corby bought a steamer and began buying and selling grain in the area between Belleville and Kingston. This trade led him to build a grist mill, and later a distillery, on the Moira River, which runs through Belleville. The Belleville authorities opposed him damming the Moira River for his mill, so he moved six kilometres upriver, just north of the town. Corby's new mill opened in 1857, and the village that grew around it became known as Corbyville.

Shortly after his mill opened, the six-foot-tall Corby, known for his rumbling voice, became mayor of Belleville for a two-year term. He was also on the board of the police commissioners and captain of the local fire company. Later, the popular politician became the Liberal member of the provincial parliament for East Hastings.

By the time of Henry Corby's death, in 1881, the fame of his whisky had spread well beyond the Belleville area. Corby's son Henry Jr.

took over after his father's death. He modernized the distillery, raising the company to a position of world prominence. Henry Jr. took a modern approach to marketing. While the father had been content to sell his whisky to local farmers by the barrel, the son saw the advantages of bottling it and expanding its market. Henry Jr. built a warehouse in Belleville, where he aged and bottled Corby whisky. He also imported wines, tobacco, and Scotch whisky. Henry Jr. was also active in politics, but as a Conservative, not a Liberal. He was later named to the Senate.

In 1905 a young tobacco salesman by the name of Mortimer Davis

Corby's mill and distillery at
Corbyville, north of Belleville,
Ontario, ca. 1870

Cattle barns near Henry
Corby's distillery. Like other
distillers of the time, Corby
fattened cattle on spent grain
mash.

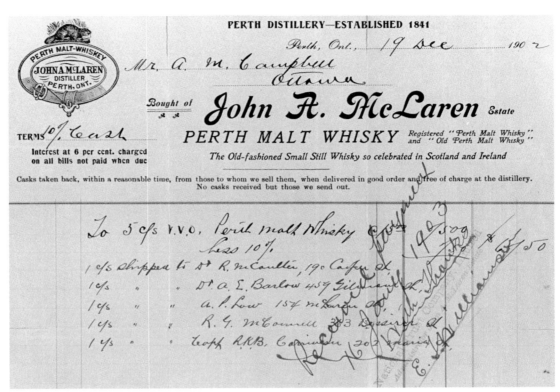

Invoice from John McLaren's distillery

bought the Corby distillery. Davis, who later founded the Imperial Tobacco Company and the Canadian Industrial Alcohol Company, was eventually knighted for his industrial and philanthropic contributions to the British Empire.

Unfortunately, the Corby distillery languished in the early years of the twentieth century. By 1921, sales had declined to a mere five hundred gallons a month. Ironically, American Prohibition brought the company back to life. Davis hired a local hotel-

owner, Harry Hatch, as sales manager in 1921. By developing connections with the smuggling world, Hatch soon had Corby sales up to fifty thousand gallons a month. Davis increased the size of the distillery, and, for a time, Corby was one of the largest distilleries in the world.

Today the Corby distillery lies empty. The executive offices of the company, which is largely owned by the Hiram Walker–Gooderham and Worts Group, are in Montreal. The Corby legacy lives on in Belleville's

Corby Park and the Corby Public Library, which the family donated to the city.

Smaller Nineteenth-Century Distilleries

The large distilling companies along Lake Ontario and the St. Lawrence were meeting the demand of the growing markets in southern Ontario and the United States. Throughout the rest of the province, however, dozens of small regional distilleries continued to meet the local needs until the turn of the century or shortly thereafter.

The town of Perth in eastern Ontario, founded in 1817 by Scottish settlers, was an important distilling centre for eastern Ontario. Two distilleries there made a distinctive style of Scotch whisky, using wood rather than peat to dry the malt. The whisky was barrel-aged in tunnels under the town, which remain to this day.

Robert McLaren obtained a licence in 1839 for a forty-gallon copper pot still. McLaren's distillery specialized in pure malt whisky with the brand names "V.V.O." and "Old Perth Malt Whisky." Records show that a Robert McLaren was employed by the Molsons in their Montreal distillery in the 1830s. This may well be the man who later established the McLaren distillery in Perth. It was subsequently run by his son John.

The other Perth company was Spalding & Stewart, which operated a Perth distillery from the 1860s to 1916, producing Old Perth and Mountain Dew Scotch whiskies. "There is not a headache in a barrel of it," was the proud claim of a Spalding & Stewart whisky ad in the *Perth Courier* of the 1880s.

John McLaren's distillery, Perth

The headaches for distillers came instead from the rise in temperance agitation. The politically powerful Temperance Movement was the final straw for Ontario's small distilleries. When the province passed the Ontario Temperance Act in 1916, McLaren's distillery and Spalding & Stewart both closed their doors.

The Spalding & Stewart distillery, Perth, Ontario. The Perth distillers aged their whisky in underground tunnels, which still exist today.

200 Henry Reifel

Henry Reifel was a German brewmaster who immigrated to British Columbia in 1888. Reifel established the British Columbia Breweries with his brothers and his son George. The company operated breweries in Nanaimo, Victoria, and Vancouver as well as liquor stores that sold Scotch malt whisky blended with Canadian spirits.

The Reifels entered the distilling business when they acquired a small distillery at New Westminster, British Columbia, originally established by a Scottish settler named William Braid. After this business was purchased by the Reifel family, it grew to the point that it could compete with eastern distillers for the West Coast trade. The company was renamed the British Columbia Distillery Company Ltd. Before long, another West Coast distillery — United Distillers of Vancouver — was competing with the Reifels. The West Coast producers made large quantities of bourbon-style whisky and exported it to the United States during Prohibition, using Tahiti as their "official" destination.

The British Columbia Distillery Company was eventually purchased by the Bronfman family, in its move to build up stocks of ageing whisky in time for the repeal of Prohibition. The purchase also included the Calvert distillery, which the Reifels had built in Amherstburg, Ontario.

Henry Reifel's British Columbia Distillers Corporation in Vancouver provided West Coast customers with Canadian whisky.

$\text{\textbf{200}}$ Whisky

Marketing in the Nineteenth Century

In the days of the pioneer, whisky was sold in bulk, in unbranded barrels or jugs. It was an agricultural product, no more identified with its producer than were beef and flour. Pioneer whisky was clear and colourless, but, around 1860, distillers began adding caramel colouring, possibly to imitate brandy, a drink popular with the upper classes.

Hiram Walker and Joseph E. Seagram were among the first Canadian distillers to give their whisky brand names and sell it in bottles. Walker's Canadian Club, first sold in the United States in 1884, and Seagram's '83 and V.O. are still popular today, over a hundred years later.

Walker was clever when it came to marketing. He realized that the best whiskies were found in exclusive men's clubs, so in 1884 he created his "Club" whisky. The brand soon became popular in Canada and the United States. But whisky makers in the United States took exception to Walker's whisky going into the United States with no mention of its country of origin. They lobbied for a law ruling that imported whisky must state its country of origin on the label. Hence "Club" whisky became "Canadian Club," or "C.C." The new law may have backfired on the U.S. whisky makers. C.C.'s status as an imported whisky actually increased its allure among American whisky drinkers, much to the disappointment of the petitioners. In 1910, Canadian Club was Canada's top export whisky.

Several unscrupulous American whisky manufacturers tried to take advantage of Walker's success. A rash of low-quality whiskies, bearing the name "Club" and stating on the label that they were made in Canada, began to appear on the market. By 1900 there were forty-two Club Whisky

Hiram Walker stencilled the word "Canadian" onto the labels of his Club whisky after U.S. distillers lobbied for legislation requiring imported whisky to state its country of origin on the label. Thus the name "Canadian Club" was born.

Seagram products from the turn of the century. (From The Seagram Museum Collection)

imitations in the United States, and sales of Canadian Club had dropped by 30 per cent. Walker countered with newspaper ads and billboards in major cities throughout the country, advertising the names of the fraudulent producers and warning consumers to avoid their products.

In their eulogy to Hiram Walker in 1899, the *Detroit News* summed up his approach to marketing as follows:

Mr. Walker began to advertise in that judicious and permanent fashion characteristic of the British manufacturers of great staples, which does not seek so much to shock the public for a day or a week, as to increase from year to year a fixed impression regarding the advertised article. ... Wherever you ask for American whisky to-day, in Europe, Asia or Africa, you are offered not Yankee spirits, but Walker Club. It is as staple as Cross & Blackwell's pickles. You can drink it in Paris, London, St. Petersburg, Berlin, Singapore, Trincamalee, Hong Kong, and in the interior of South Africa. It has even made its way into the United States, and has overcome with many the natural American taste for Bourbon and American Rye.[13]

When several U.S. distillers imitated the look and the name of Canadian Club, Walker fought back aggressively with billboard campaigns in several major U.S. cities.

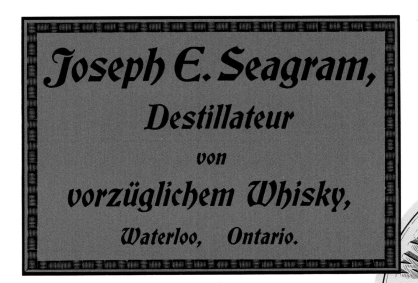

Joseph Seagram placed this ad in a German almanac to reach the large German population in Waterloo.

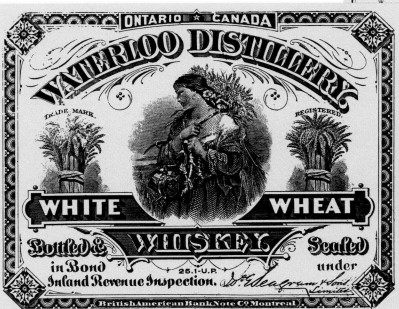

Some of Joseph Seagram's early labels were printed by the British American Bank Note Company.

Whiskies of the World

There are four traditional whiskies: Scotch, Irish, bourbon, and Canadian. By international agreement, Scotch is made only in Scotland, Canadian whisky only in Canada, and so on. But the situation is changing. Japanese whisky, which resembles Scotch in its manufacturing process, grows more important, while the amount of Irish whisky sold keeps it out of the top one hundred brands. The *International Drinks Bulletin* keeps track of the world's one hundred top-selling brands of all spirits. To be included, a brand must sell one million or more nine-litre cases (i.e., twelve 750-mL bottles) a year. In 1992, whisky accounted for sales of 98.1 million cases. The breakdown follows:

Scotch	44.2	million
Canadian	17.2	,,
Japanese	17.1	,,
Bourbon	12.5	,,
American	5.4	,,
Spanish	1.7	,,

Scotch Whisky

Blended Scotch whisky is a blend of aged single-malt whiskies made in pot stills with aged grain whiskies made in column stills. Single malt Scotch is an unblended whisky made entirely from malted barley, by one distiller, in traditional pot stills. Be it blended or single, all Scotch whiskies have a unique smoky flavour that comes from the Scottish custom of drying the malt over a smoky peat fire. All Scotch whisky must be aged in casks for at least three years.

Irish Whiskey*

Irish whiskey is made with about 40 per cent malted barley and 60 per cent unmalted barley. Peat fires are not used to dry the malt, so Irish whiskey has a clear, malty flavour, and none of the smokiness of Scotch. Being triple-distilled, Irish whiskey has a higher proof and therefore tastes milder than single-malt Scotch. Irish whiskey must remain in casks for at least three years.

The Longmorn-Glenlivet distillery near Elgin in Scotland's Speyside whisky region

American Whiskey*

American blended whisky is a blend of at least 20 per cent bourbon or another small-grain straight whisky, and either aged light whisky (similar to Canadian base whisky) or unaged grain neutral spirits. The minimum age of the straight whiskies in the blend is two years. If the age of the blend is less than four years, a label statement must say so.

Bourbon

Bourbon is a straight (unblended) whisky, similar to Scotch single malt whisky. It was first made about 1780 in Bourbon County, Kentucky; hence the name. The principal ingredient of bourbon is corn, which, by law, must make up between 51 and 80 per cent of the mash bill. Various grains make up the rest. Bourbon must age in new, charred, oak barrels for at least two years.

Tennessee whiskey is a particular type of bourbon that must seep slowly through vats of charcoal to mellow. There are just two brands: Jack Daniels and George Dickel.

Canadian Whisky

Canadian whisky is a blend of a light-bodied base whisky and heavier flavouring whiskies. The main flavouring element is rye. Canadian whiskies are lighter in flavour and character than other whiskies, because of different techniques of distilling, maturing, and blending. Both the flavouring and the base whisky in Canadian whisky must age at least three years, and usually age longer.

Japanese Whisky

The Japanese have been producing whisky since the 1920s, mainly for their own consumption. They make both single malt and blended whiskies in the Scottish style, even using peat in the malting process. They also import Scotch malt whisky for blending. Japan's distilleries are large and modern. By far the biggest producer is Suntory.

* The Irish and the Americans spell whiskey with an "e." Canadians and Scots spell it without the "e."

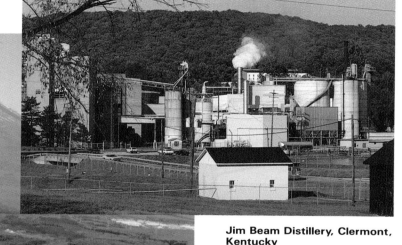

Jim Beam Distillery, Clermont, Kentucky

Kirin-Seagram distillery at the foot of Mount Fuji, Japan

CHAPTER 4
Early Distilling Technology in Canada

From earth and sun and rain are born
The mellow barley, rye and corn.
Then, Man steps in, with wisdom old,
Distills the grain to liquid gold.
This nectar, then, they age and blend
And bottle ... to the worthy end,
That you may drink the deep delight
Of whiskey that is truly right!
Purveyor, dealer, barman, too ...
Each plays his part in serving you
The harmony that all men seek,
Of Nature's bounty ... Man's technique.

*– Found on a label of Harmony Blended
Whiskey, made by Carstairs Bros.
Distilling Co., Inc.*

From Pot Still to Column Still

Until the mid-1800s, whisky making on both sides of the Atlantic was a hit-and-miss affair. All whisky was made in batches, in traditional onion-shaped copper pot stills. Considerable differences appeared from one batch to another. Frequent bad batches were blamed on "a change of the moon" or other natural events. There was no such thing as a hydrometer for determining the alcoholic content of whisky, and the make-up of the distillate, with its impurities, or "congeners," was but vaguely understood. Distillers knew that malted barley played a critical role in whisky making, but they weren't sure why.

With the coming of the Industrial Revolution, many processes underwent improvement and streamlining, and distilling was one of them. Scottish and Irish distillers began experimenting to develop a new distillation apparatus in the late eighteenth century. They produced an entirely new type of still: a vertical column that distilled continuously rather than in batches.

Before examining the differences between pot and column stills, one needs to understand the basic procedure for making whisky. The first steps are the same as those followed in making beer: cleaned grain is ground and mixed with hot water. Malt is added, and the mixture, known as the mash, is allowed to cook for several hours. During the mashing, enzymes from the malt transform the starch in the grain to fermentable sugars. The mixture is then cooled, and yeast is added. The yeast converts the sugar to alcohol and carbon dioxide during the process of fermentation.

The fermented mash, referred to as "beer" by North American distillers, is now sent to the still. Heat is applied, the beer begins to boil, producing vapour. Since alcohol has a lower boiling point than water, it evaporates first. It rises to the top of the pot and enters a condenser, or "worm" (the term comes from its long, coiled shape), where the vapour condenses back into liquid. The stillman uses a hydrometer to take regular measurements of the liquid coming out of the condenser. When the specific gravity of the vapour is close to 1.000 (the specific gravity of water), he stops the

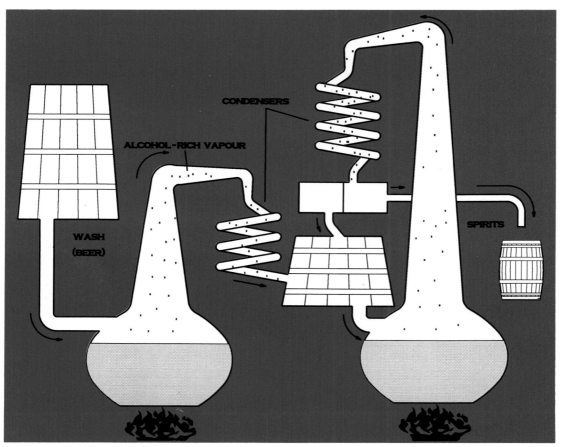

In a pot still, whisky is produced by the batch and the product is high in flavour and congener content.

process. The material left in the bottom of the still is removed and made into a nutritious livestock feed called "distillers' dried grains."

This first distilling produces "low wines" that are weak in alcohol. In the second distillation, which produces "high wines," the first portion to come off is the foreshot, or "heads." The stillman prevents this milky liquid, which is high in the low-boiling congeners (aldehydes and methanol), from running into the spirit receiver. When the spirit runs clear, he or she diverts it into the spirit receiver. The final part of the run, known as "feints" or "tails," also contains undesirable compounds — the higher-boiling fusel oils — that must be removed from the distillate. When the specific gravity reaches a certain point indicating that the tails have been reached, the stillman again redirects the flow of spirits so that it does not go into the spirit receiver.

This two-step distillation process produces raw spirits still quite heavy in congeners. Single malt whiskies have been produced by this method, in pot stills, for centuries. They are still made this way in Ireland and Scotland.

Excessively high concentrations of congeners make whisky undrinkable. In lesser concentrations they give whisky flavour; the more congeners, the longer the whisky needs to be aged and the more flavourful will be the final product. Canadian whisky is a blend of base whisky,

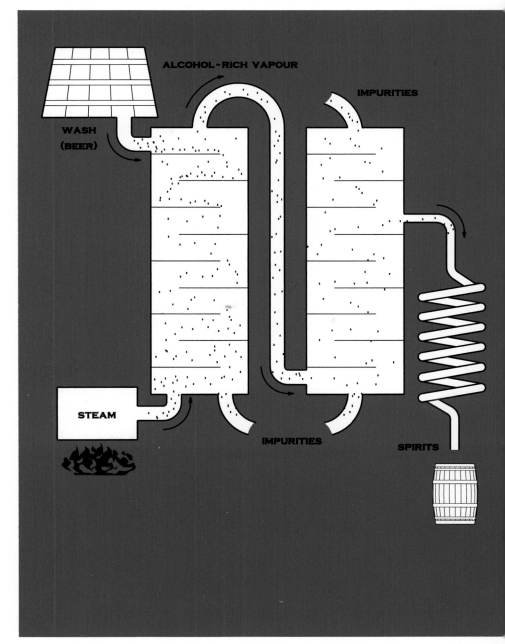

A column still continuously produces a purer and less flavourful whisky.

which has had almost all of the congeners removed (and is about 96 per cent alcohol by volume), and flavouring whiskies, which have a higher congener content. Flavouring whiskies are similar to the single malt whiskies in character.

Blended whisky was developed as a result of the new column stills, with their improved ability to produce a much lighter-flavoured whisky. Column stills first appeared in Scotland in 1826. A few years later, an Irish excise officer by the name of Aeneas Coffey made further improvements to the first column still. The Coffey still, invented in 1832, features two columns: a beer still and a rectifying, or secondary distillation, column. The Coffey still distills the beer and rectifies the distillate into a light-flavoured, continuous type whisky. The stillman introduces the beer at the top of the still, and it descends via a series of perforated plates to the bottom. Steam is introduced at the bottom of the beer still. As the steam rises it strips the alcohol from the beer.

The Coffey still rendered whisky making more efficient, and gave distillers better control of the final product by allowing them to control the temperature along the column. Because the various flavour components of whisky vapourize at different temperatures, being able to remove components as they reach their individual boiling points gave distillers much more control. Coffey stills are still used today. At Seagram, for example, distillers use the product of the Coffey still primarily as a special blending whisky, like a flavouring whisky.

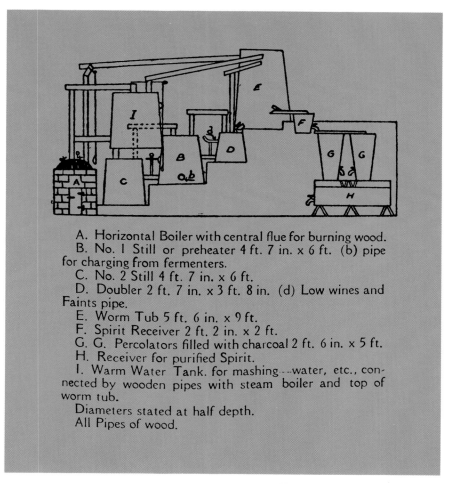

A. Horizontal Boiler with central flue for burning wood.
B. No. 1 Still or preheater 4 ft. 7 in. x 6 ft. (b) pipe for charging from fermenters.
C. No. 2 Still 4 ft. 7 in. x 6 ft.
D. Doubler 2 ft. 7 in. x 3 ft. 8 in. (d) Low wines and Faints pipe.
E. Worm Tub 5 ft. 6 in. x 9 ft.
F. Spirit Receiver 2 ft. 2 in. x 2 ft.
G. G. Percolators filled with charcoal 2 ft. 6 in. x 5 ft.
H. Receiver for purified Spirit.
I. Warm Water Tank. for mashing---water, etc., connected by wooden pipes with steam boiler and top of worm tub.
Diameters stated at half depth.
All Pipes of wood.

A pot still on display at The Seagram Museum in Waterloo, Ontario. The wooden tank on the left would have contained a coiled condensing unit surrounded by cold water. The alcohol-rich vapour from the still would flow through the coil and condense into whisky, which then flowed into the copper spirit safe below.

This illustration of a distillery near York (Toronto) shows a typical, though small, early Canadian distilling arrangement.

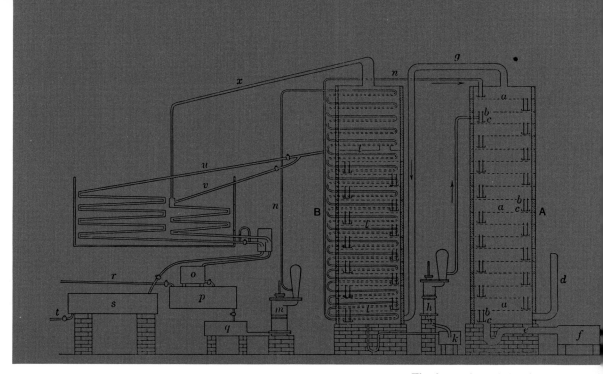

The invention of the Coffey still (shown above) by Irish excise officer Aeneas Coffey in 1832 revolutionized distilling. Coffey stills led to the development of blended whiskies.

When John Molson established his Montreal distillery in 1799, column stills were not yet available, so the Molsons began with pot stills, switching to column stills later. When Gooderham and Worts set up their distillery in 1837, they purchased wooden column stills, which were most popular in North America at the time. These wooden column stills, which were made in Canada, didn't have the sophistication of the Coffey still with its perforated metal plates.

Instead, Gooderham and Worts packed their stills with cobblestones to provide a surface on which steam and beer could meet. As historian E.B. Shuttleworth put it, "One can easily conceive that an uprushing current of steam, meeting with 'beer' in its descending passage over and between the cobble stones, would quickly be deprived of its alcoholic contents, though in a rather crude manner."[14]

By this time distillers also began to understand more about the make-up of whisky, and what needed to be removed from the distillate in order to make it palatable. Much effort was directed at removing the fusel oil, which was more of a problem with whisky made from wheat than from the more traditional barley and malt.

In the 1830s, the better North American whisky makers were rectifying or purifying their spirits to remove fusel oil, not through secondary distillation as is done today but by filtering the whisky through charcoal or charred bone dust. When Thomas Molson visited New York distilleries in 1836, he wrote in his diary: "... saw Distillery and 40 rectifying charcoal tubs made of pine, 6 feet diameter each, & wooden stills for running spirits from charcoal of rectifiers by Steam."[15]

Mashing room at Gooderham and Worts. Here, ground grain was mixed with hot water and malt to bring about the conversion of starch to fermentable sugars.

Rectifying room at Gooderham and Worts. At this time (the 1860s), rectifying involved filtering the whisky through charcoal or charred bone dust.

Still room at Gooderham and Worts. These wooden stills would have been made in Canada. Note the primitive instrument controls and spirit safe on the right.

Gooderham and Worts appears to have begun rectifying its whisky with charcoal in 1838 — the first year in which the purchase of charcoal appears in the company's books. A report on the new Gooderham and Worts distillery in the *Toronto Globe* describes the plant's forty-two rectifiers, each with a capacity of eight hundred gallons and filled with powdered charcoal through which the whisky slowly filtered. The charcoal, the writer adds, has to be renewed every six to eight months.

Along with the charcoal rectifiers, Gooderham and Worts was also, by 1862, sending its whisky through a secondary distillation to remove even more of the congeners. The whisky was pumped through underground pipes into the old windmill tower. There, two new copper column stills, each with a capacity of 1500 gallons, had been installed for the second distillation. At some point about this time, the practice of charcoal filtering ceased. Gooderham and Worts had obviously discovered that it could control the chemical make-up of its whisky entirely through secondary distillation.

Hiram Walker also purified his whisky with charcoal, but he also used a few other materials:

The rectifiers were constructed in the following manner: A few inches above the true bottom of the casks was a perforated bottom. Upon this bottom a woolen blanket or a cleanly-carded cotton was spread, then came a stratum of gravel or pebbles the size of large peas. Upon this was placed six inches of charcoal, then a layer of barley malt, and again charcoal up to a foot and a half from the top; then another woolen blanket, and another layer of gravel and finally more charcoal to within eight inches of the top. These rectifiers were placed in series, every one being connected with the next succeeding one by means of a faucet, until the liquid finally reached the common reservoir at the bottom.[16]

Walker's efforts at purification of his product might bring smiles to the faces of distillers today. But even in the early days of the Walker distillery, its whisky enjoyed a reputation for extremely high purity. Later, Hiram Walker invented and patented a new multiple-column distillation technique, which the company still uses today. The multi-column unit consists of an extraction column, an alcohol column, and a recovery column. Whisky from the beer still is fed into the multiple-column still continuously, and the draw-off of heads, centres, and tails is carried out simultaneously.

When this photo was taken in 1918, Gooderham and Worts had replaced some of their wooden fermenting tuns, or tanks, with stainless steel tuns.

Michael Jackson, the British whisky connoisseur who wrote the 1987 *World Guide to Whisky*, credits Hiram Walker with being responsible for a national style of whisky for Canada:

> Because of his distinctive method of production, subsequently adopted by all the country's distillers, Canadian Club managed to combine some of the full flavour of North American whiskies — especially the fruitiness — with a much cleaner and lighter, perhaps crisper, palate than was common at the time. These characteristics have been associated with Canadian whiskies ever since.[17]

Was Hiram Walker the first to blend neutral spirits with flavouring whiskies to create the first true Canadian whisky? It may have been Walker or Joseph E. Seagram, or it could have been Gooderham and Worts. Perhaps the latter was producing neutral spirits in the stone windmill tower overlooking Lake Ontario in 1862. If so, they may have blended it with more flavourful whiskies. Wherever blending began, there is no doubt that it caught on among Canadian distillers. By the 1880s, both Joseph E. Seagram and Hiram Walker were marketing blended whisky throughout North America. Seagram's '83 was a blend, as was Walker's Club Whisky, introduced to the American market in 1884.

It must have been a matter of pride for those distillers whose equipment and technique allowed them to eliminate the foul-tasting fusel oil. Joseph E. Seagram's grandson told a story of a bartender opening a new bottle of Seagram's '83 for his grandfather one day: Before opening the bottle, the bartender began shaking it. Bartenders in those days were in the habit of shaking up whisky bottles to distribute the fusel oil that would normally have risen to the top. Annoyed, Seagram told the bartender that this was not necessary with his whisky — the fusel oil had been removed.

New fermenters at Gooderham and Worts

The "Whisky War"

The issues of blended versus straight whiskies, and fusel oil content, initiated a "whisky war" between U.S. and Canadian distillers in 1909, a war that was not to be resolved until President Howard Taft finally answered the question, "What *is* whisky?"

In 1906, after the U.S. Congress passed a Pure Food Law, American distillers lobbied Washington to have straight whisky recognized as the only whisky. In other words, those made by blending neutral spirits with flavouring whiskies — the whiskies of Canada — should be deprived of recognition as a pure food in the United States and hence be outlawed in that country.

Despite the fact that straight whisky contains fusel oil, the U.S. distillers managed to convince the chief government chemist and the solicitor general of their point. In 1908, Canadian Club and presumably all other types of blended Canadian whisky were refused entry into the United States. Existing stocks were seized by authorities and removed from the market.

Hiram Walker and Sons appealed to the U.S. Supreme Court. A temporary injunction was granted, and a complete inquiry into the whisky controversy began. In 1910, President Taft quoted from the inquiry report in handing down his decision

— one of great importance for the future of the Canadian whisky industry:

> Whisky, for more than one hundred years, had been the most general and comprehensive term applied to liquor distilled from grain. ... Its flavor and color have varied with the changes in the process of its manufacture in the United States, Ireland, Scotland and England. ... The efforts of those engaged in the manufacture were directed toward the reduction of the amount of Fusel Oil in the product. ...
>
> It was supposed for a long time that by ageing of Straight Whisky in the charred wood a chemical change took place which rid the liquor of Fusel Oil. ... It now appears by chemical analysis that this is untrue; that the effect of the ageing is only to dissipate the odor, and to modify the raw, unpleasant flavor, but to leave the Fusel Oil still in the Straight Whisky. ...
>
> After an examination of all the evidence, it seems to me overwhelmingly established that for a hundred years the term Whisky in the trade and among the customers, has included all potable liquor distilled from grain.[18]

Taft's decision made it clear: whisky was whisky, whether blended or straight. American straight whisky producers would have to compete with the smoother, and increasingly popular, blended whisky being produced by their neighbours to the north.

The Invention of the Hydrometer

Distillers in both the Old World and the New had no way of determining the strength of their whisky until Englishman Benjamin Sykes invented the hydrometer in the 1790s. Home beer and wine makers are familiar with this simple tool, which measures the strength of alcohol by determining its specific gravity. The use of hydrometers became law in Britain's distilling industry in 1818, and in Canada's in 1846. It was essential not only to the stillman, for gauging the strength of the alcohol during distillation, but also to the excise officer, who used it to confirm the alcohol content of each distillation, before and after distilled water was added to bring the whisky to the desired concentration of alcohol: 40 per cent.

Before the hydrometer was invented, the accepted way to test the alcohol content of a spirit was to mix it with gunpowder and ignite it. This practice was the origin of the term "proof." If the distiller could ignite the whisky mixture, that was "proof" of alcohol content. If it didn't burn, the whisky was "under-proof." If it burned too vigorously, it was "over-proof." The gunpowder method was highly inaccurate, and the development of the hydrometer was a major step forward in the production of all sorts of alcoholic beverages. Inaccurate or not, though, the term "proof" is still widely used today.

The Origins of Whisky Ageing in Canada

By about 1840, distillers commonly made whisky continuously rather than in batches; they purified it through rectification in charcoal and through secondary distillation; and they regularly measured its strength. The industry was beginning to take on a modern look, but one big element remained to be changed: unlike their counterparts in Scotland and Ireland, North American distillers were not yet ageing their whisky.

As with the origins of blending, the origins of ageing whisky in Canada are hazy. All distillers had to age their whisky by law, as of 1890. In that year, the Dominion government brought the Two Year Maturing Law into effect, requiring distillers to age their whisky in oak barrels of 150-gallon capacity or less for at least two years before selling it. The new law spelled the end for many small distilleries, and compelled the large ones to build extensive storage warehouses. (The two years was increased to three in 1974.)

However, the distillers knew well before 1890 that ageing improved the taste of whisky, and the big distillers began ageing their best whiskies well before they were required to by law. But they also produced cheaper brands that were aged very little, if at all. Gooderham and Worts produced both a "common" whisky, aged from two to twelve months, and higher quality spirits, such as Old Rye, that were aged longer. Joseph E. Seagram probably began ageing his Seagram's '83 in sherry casks by at least 1880. He may have aged other whiskies earlier.

Yeast container, copper and brass, Canadian, 1940–60. (From The Seagram Museum Collection)

Mash sampler, copper and brass, American. (From The Seagram Museum Collection)

The hydrometer, used to measure specific gravity, and hence alcohol content, of a liquid, is an essential tool for both distiller and excise officer.

With each year of maturing, the barrel imparts a bit more of its tannin and colour to the whisky. (From The Seagram Museum Collection)

Charring the interior of the barrels opens the pores of the wood, speeding up the maturing process and adding colour to the whisky.

This barrel warehouse at the
Hiram Walker distillery in
Walkerville, Ontario, illustrates
rack storage, with barrels laid
on their sides. Today, barrels
are usually stored on pallets, in
a vertical position.

Used in Canadian Whisky

Today, corn is the major ingredient of Canadian whisky, making up about 80 per cent of the mash bill. But it wasn't always so. Any small grain — wheat, oats, rye, barley, or corn — can be used to make whisky. Early Canadian distillers would have used whatever grains were available, commonly wheat and rye. "Middlings" — larger pieces of all sorts of grain left over from the flour milling process — were an important component, which shows that in the early days distillers were not fussy about the make-up of their mash bill.

Canadians grew corn only experimentally in 1840, but by 1843 corn had become an increasingly important ingredient in Gooderham and Worts's whisky. That year, a typical mash recipe called for 20 bushels of chop (a mix of rough-cut grains of all sorts), 17 1/2 bushels of corn, 82 pounds of rye, and 80 pounds of malt. As the years went by, the middlings and chop in the mash bills decreased while corn increased. Corn yields one-third more starch per bushel than wheat or rye, so distillers would have favoured it for economic reasons.

The record books of 1859 show that distillers in the Leeds and Grenville counties, which would have included Wiser, used the following amounts of grain (in bushels): malt, 5107; wheat, 5584; barley, 64; rye,

21 003; corn, 42 745; buckwheat, 385; and oats, 5335. The proportion of corn used has grown to the point that today it makes up about 80 per cent of the grain that goes into Canadian whisky. Rye, the main flavouring grain, is used in both raw and malt forms, as is barley.

One cannot make whisky without malt. This essential ingredient contains a complex of enzymes, collectively called "diastase," that con-

verts the starch in grain to sugars, which the yeast can then ferment. For Canada's early distillers, malt was a precious commodity that had to be produced in specialized malt houses. Necessity being the mother of invention, the pioneer distillers were soon experimenting to determine how little malt they needed to add to the raw grain mash in order to convert the starch to sugar.

The milling room at Gooderham and Worts. Grain was fed down pipes to the millstones for grinding.

CHAPTER 5
The Temperance Movement and Prohibition in Canada

Canadian historian Graeme Decarie wrote that Prohibition was, "a long time coming in Canada, and a short time going."[19] Prohibition sentiment grew and gained momentum all over the country from the 1820s, when the Temperance Movement began in Canada, to the 1920s, when provincially operated liquor stores took over the distribution and sale of alcohol. But, although individual provinces, notably Ontario, did enforce Prohibition successfully for a decade or more, full country-wide Prohibition was over almost as soon as it began. It lasted only from March 1918 to December 1919.

Beginning in the 1850s, the question of whether or not to make Canada "dry" was continually in the headlines. The issue was debated as hotly as free trade and Sunday shopping are debated in the 1990s. Temperance sentiment fueled huge demonstrations. The issue caused extensive antagonism between federal and provincial governments and

generated floods of fervent broadsides and posters, fiery rhetoric, and religious fervour. For nearly one hundred years, the liquor traffic was Canada's most hotly discussed social issue.

We have already seen some effects of temperance agitation on distillers. On the one hand, the Molsons gave up the distilling business in 1867, partly in response to the Temperance Movement, which frowned particularly on distilled spirits. On the other hand, Hiram Walker and J.P. Wiser both came to Canada from the United States partly because the Temperance Movement had not yet reached the degree of activity in Canada that it had in the United States. They were in for a surprise. Temperance agitators on both sides of the border aided and abetted one another's efforts, sharing their speakers, publications, and posters back and forth as needed. Distillers would have to put up with looking like villains — in some eyes at least — for close to a century.

The Origins of the Temperance Movement

The Temperance Movement began in Canada in 1827 and 1828, about the same time that similar movements were developing in the United States, Britain, and northern Europe. The first meetings took place in Nova Scotia, the eastern townships of Quebec, and in Montreal. By 1832 there were close to one hundred temperance societies in Upper Canada with ten thousand members. By 1842, one Upper Canadian in ten was a member. Thousands, many of them children, had signed pledge cards.

The Temperance Movement was a response to the widespread abuse of alcohol, but it also went beyond that issue. Temperance grew out of a larger social phenomenon known as the social gospel movement, which applied Christian values and solutions to the troubles of an industrializing society. The social gospel

Pledge cards were signed by thousands of Canadian men, women, and children during the nearly one-hundred-year life of the Temperance Movement.

A temperance meeting in Toronto

movement took hold in Canada in the 1880s, a time of political corruption, economic hardship, and increasing urban disorder. Through the movement, churches encouraged their members to become more involved in solving social problems and in agitating for legislation to better society.

When communities were small and community members knew one another, social structures were in place to prevent rampant alcoholism. But the disruptive effects of industrialization and urbanization changed society in ways that contributed to an increase in alcohol abuse. Industrial productivity declined, the number of alcohol-related accidents increased, and family life was threatened with alcohol-induced

61

violence. Alcohol was seen as a major cause of poverty and sickness; many felt it was time to bring the problem under control.

In the Upper and Lower Canada of the early 1800s, many of the social niceties that we take for granted today — concerts, plays, and club activities — didn't exist. Temperance organizations changed that. They held picnics, concerts, lectures, and outings of all sorts. They built Temperance Halls, providing an alternative to the ever-present tavern, as venues for social gatherings. Temperance hotels provided the first alternative to the early inns that invariably grew up around the taverns, though most of these dry establishments failed by the end of the 1860s, mainly due to a lack of revenue from liquor sales.

The earliest temperance societies were moderate in their approach to alcohol. They promoted temperance — not total abstinence — and believed that the decision to drink or not was up to the individual. Wine, beer, and cider were acceptable, but the societies encouraged their members to stay away from "hard liquor." Perhaps early temperance agitators felt the chances of getting people to give up the age-old habit of drinking beer were slight. But by the 1840s the movement was heating up. The "old pledge" societies were gradually replaced by more political, more militant anti-alcohol organizations. Members became obsessed with the evils of alcohol, and civilized cultural events gave way to marches and confrontations. Moderation pledges were replaced with total abstinence pledges. Those who signed these *total* abstinence pledges became known as "teetotallers."

The WCTU and the Dominion Alliance

The Women's Christian Temperance Union (WCTU) got underway in Canada in 1874, with meetings in Owen Sound and Picton, Ontario. Membership grew to over eleven thousand members by 1911, and to nearly double that by 1929. Women were "modern" if they belonged to the WCTU.

Temperance organizations produced many posters creatively advocating temperance sentiments.

ALCOHO

A BLESSING

A CURSE

GOOD FOR THE ENGINE, BUT NOT FOR TH ENGINEER

GOOD FOR COMMERCIAL PURPOSES, BUT NOT AS A BEV

A Temperance Hall in Oakville, Ontario, built in 1843

One woman emerged as the main force of the union in Canada. Founder and president of the Ontario WCTU, Letitia Youmans, a former teacher, lived with her husband on their farm in Picton, Ontario. She was a good speaker, an excellent writer, and a great organizer, creating the Ontario WCTU almost single-handedly. Described by her American counterpart, Frances Willard, as a woman of "ample avoirdupois," Youmans was a fiery orator who converted thousands of people to the cause.

Youmans believed whole-heartedly in the power of education. She was convinced that if children were taught the evils of drink at an early age, society's alcohol problem would disappear as they grew up. She organized the "Little Band of Hope,"

which was a group of young temperance fighters. The WCTU lobbied hard to have scientific temperance instruction as part of school curriculum. They also promoted domestic arts training in the schools, which led to the development of home economics courses for girls.

In 1876, two years after the Canadian WCTU was founded, the Dominion Alliance for the Total Suppression of the Liquor Traffic was born. An umbrella organization for dozens of smaller temperance societies, the alliance became the major temperance lobby for the next fifty years.

Who were the typical temperance agitators in Canada? They were both men and women. One tends to think that women played a larger role than men, probably because of the work

Letitia Youmans, a rousing speaker and energetic organizer, was the first president of the Canadian Women's Christian Temperance Union.

HELP US! WE WOULD CLOSE THE SALOO

Temperance agitators believed that if children were taught the evils of drink, they would grow up to be non-drinkers. These children are from the Hillhurst Presbyterian Sunday school group, Calgary, ca. 1912–16.

of the WCTU, but, in fact, men were equally involved. In the very early days of the movement, women were not even allowed to attend the meetings.

The typical temperance agitators were middle-class, rural dwellers rather than urbanites. Most cities voted "wet" in the numerous referenda on the issue, even though the leaders and money for campaigns came mainly from the cities. Fraternal societies, such as the Knight Templars of Temperance, Sons of Temperance, and Knights of Temperance, were important forces in promoting the movement in small towns. With their rituals, parades, and military-inspired uniforms and medals, these lodges had enormous influence.

Finally, a typical temperance agitator was likely to be a Methodist or a member of one of the other Protestant fundamentalist religions: Presbyterian, Baptist, and Episcopal. Anglicans and Catholics did not embrace temperance sentiments to the same degree.

The Temperance Movement Across Canada

Attitudes towards temperance varied greatly from one province to the next. On the one hand, in the Maritime provinces pro-temperance sentiment was strong. New Brunswick was the first province in Canada to vote in Prohibition, albeit for only a

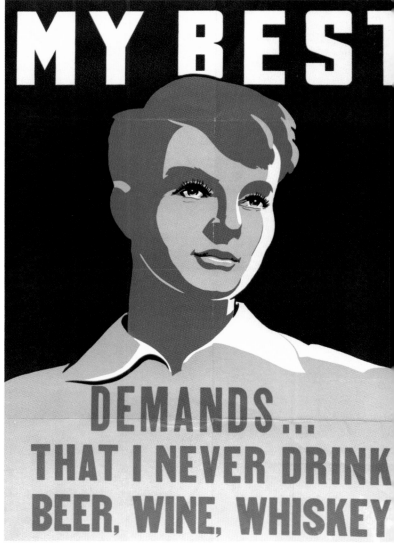

The Ontario Temperance Federation prepared this temperance poster for the United Church of Canada, ca. 1925. (From The Seagram Museum Collection)

short time, in 1856. It had been influenced by events in Maine, a neighbouring state that was an important early temperance stronghold in the United States. Prince Edward Island also voted in Prohibition in 1901.

Quebec, on the other hand, steadfastly held out against total prohibition of alcohol. Quebecers did express some temperance sentiments, and one of Canada's most notorious agitators, Father Charles Chiniquy, was based in Montreal. But while many Quebecers were in favour of eliminating distilled spirits, few had any interest in giving up beer and wine. This was at least partly owing to the influence of the Catholic church in Quebec, wine being essential to the Catholic sacrament of communion.

British artist George Cruikshank produced several illustrations depicting drinking and its effects. They were used by temperance promoters on both sides of the Atlantic.

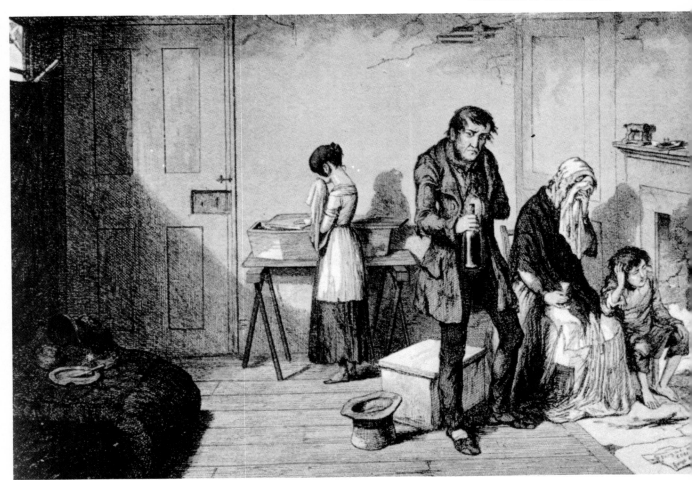

British Columbia's Temperance Movement was also weak, at least until the turn of the twentieth century. Its male-dominated population of miners, fishermen, and loggers, all involved in seasonal employment in isolated areas, may have needed the solace of liquor more than most. In any case, liquor consumption in British Columbia was nearly double the national average in the 1890s. British Columbia was the last English-speaking province to adopt Prohibition and the first to drop it, in 1921.

Although Quebec did not embrace temperance sentiment to the extent that some other provinces did, this 1917 poster shows that at least some Quebecers wanted to abolish the bar.

New Brunswick, influenced by strong temperance fervour in the neighbouring state of Maine, was the first province to vote in Prohibition. This 1890s photograph shows the WCTU's headquarters — a former army barracks in Fredericton.

Ontario provided the mainstay of the Temperance Movement in Canada; it remembered, perhaps, the heavy drinking that had been common among Upper Canada's pioneers. When the first local option law, the Dunkin Act, came into force in 1864, municipalities in Upper and Lower Canada were given the right to decide whether they would be "wet" or "dry." Much of Upper Canada went dry and stayed that way until 1927, when Ontario created its provincial liquor control board. Toronto's nickname, "Toronto the Good," is at least partly due to the city's position as the capital of a strong temperance province.

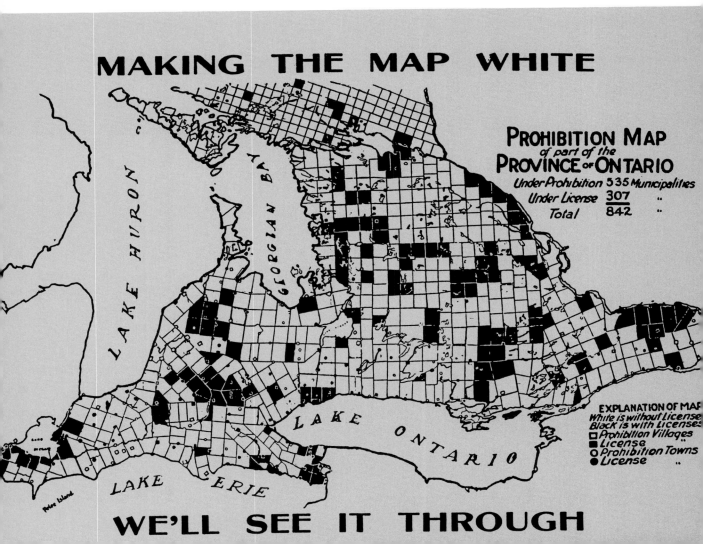

A map of Ontario showing which counties voted wet and which voted dry in 1915

Tiger Dunlop

Dr. William "Tiger" Dunlop (1792–1848), adventurer, physician, writer, and "warden of the forests" for the Canada Company, was vocal in his opposition to temperance. Dunlop travelled with his "twelve apostles": twelve glass bottles, each holding a gallon of a different spirit. One of the apostles still exists today, in the collection of the Huron County Museum in Goderich, Ontario.

> Upper Canada may be pronounced the most healthy country under the sun, considering that whisky can be procured for about one shilling sterling per gallon.[20]

Thomas Talbot

Colonel Thomas Talbot (1771–1853), an eccentric colonial official who presided over the settlement of southwestern Ontario, was known as a heavy drinker.

> Damn your calomel, pills, opium and blisters! There is my morning doctor (pointing to a cold bath in the corner of the room) and there (glancing at a bottle of whisky) is my afternoon physician. At night I sleep soundly, owing to a clear conscience, for I throw politics and Temperance lectures to the devil.[21]

Stephen Leacock

Stephen Leacock (1869–1944) was a professor of economics and political science at McGill University in Montreal, though today Canadians revere him primarily as a writer and humourist. His writings contain frequent allusions to the subject of drinking, many of them aimed directly at the temperance agitators.

> Prohibition cannot last ... because it is based upon a lie. And a lie cannot endure. Prohibition declares it to be a crime to drink beer. The common sense of every honest man tells him that it is not a crime to drink a glass of beer. ... The attempt to make the consumption of beer criminal is as silly and as futile as if you passed a law to send a man to jail for eating cucumber salad.[22]

Famous Canadian "Drys"

Among the dry proponents in the temperance debate, were Father Charles-Paschal Chiniquy, Egerton Ryerson, Ernest Drury, and Nellie Mooney McClung.

Father Chiniquy

Father Chiniquy (1809–1899) called himself "an apostle of Temperance." An acclaimed orator, he travelled throughout Quebec, establishing temperance groups and convincing hundreds of thousands of people to sign the pledge. In the end he may have done more harm than good to the Temperance Movement in Quebec: in 1856 he was excommunicated after being charged with sexual escapades, arson, and embezzlement.

> Religion and your Country are equally and deeply affected by the pernicious results of intemperance. Both sincerely lament the ruin of thousands of their children, drawn into the vortex of perdition by those pernicious liquors. Cast your eyes around, and you will be struck with awe in viewing everywhere the ruinous effects of that most debasing vice.[23]

Nellie Mooney McClung

Nellie Mooney McClung (1873–1951), a writer, teacher, and promoter of women's suffrage, also supported Prohibition.

> Prohibition is a hard sounding word, worthless as a rallying cry, hard as a locked door or going to bed without your supper. It could never fire the heather. ... The Church has given many a real vision ... but even the Church often presents a dour face, with its locked door and musty smells. ... We, the temperance women ... have to make our cause attractive. We must fight fire with fire.[24]

Ernest Drury

Ernest Drury (1878–1968), co-founder and first president of the United Farmers of Ontario, was elected premier of Ontario in 1920. One of the main accomplishments of his administration was strict enforcement of the Ontario Temperance Act, which became law in 1916.

> The present liquor law is the well-considered judgment of the people themselves, after years of discussion and experience, and its enforcement has resulted in a decrease in crime and an increase in prosperity, morality and happiness. ... There must be no turning back.[25]

As a Methodist minister and editor of the Methodist newspaper, the *Christian Monitor*, Egerton Ryerson (1803–1882) had plenty of opportunity to promote his temperance ideas. In the July 2, 1835, edition, he wrote this dramatic description of how a Connecticut temperance organization overcame the evils of alcohol, deep-rooted in their society:

> In their resolutions, we see a strange commixture of principle and error, of light and shade, showing that although conscience was at work, yet the workings were like those of the elements of nature which are imprisoned beneath the weight of mountains and continents. So the power of principle, in this instance, was crushed by the overshadowings of deep-rooted error and prejudice. It commenced at first with a low murmer, shaking but slightly the solid mass of error. Then came another shock; and finally the earthquake itself came and at once shook down the hills of prejudice, and demonstrated its feebleness to withstand principles.[26]

Egerton Ryerson

Temperance Legislation and the National Plebiscite of 1898

The growing Temperance Movement in Upper Canada resulted in legislation that reduced drinking. The difficult issue was passed on to the municipalities, just as, in recent years, the Sunday shopping issue in Ontario was passed along to the municipalities.

In 1864, three years before Confederation, the United Province of Canada (Upper and Lower Canada) passed the Dunkin Act, which allowed municipalities to vote on whether or not to allow liquor. In Upper Canada, another piece of legislation, the Crooks Act of 1876, made it more difficult to obtain a tavern licence. The Crooks Act reduced the number of taverns from nearly five thousand in 1875 to less than four thousand by 1914. Given the growth in population over those years, this reduction in the number of watering holes becomes more dramatic.

In 1878 the new Dominion government passed the Canada Temperance Act or Scott Act. This new piece of legislation extended the local option law established by the Dunkin Act to all of Canada instead of just Upper and Lower Canada. The Scott Act allowed Prohibition to be introduced by any city or county by a petition signed by one-quarter of the electors. The act dried up the

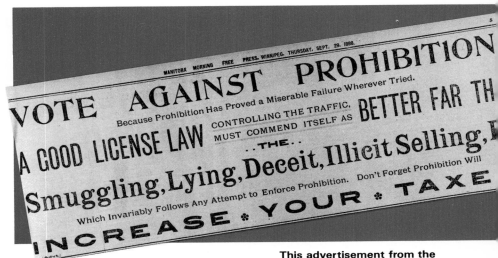

This advertisement from the *Manitoba Morning Free Press* of September 29, 1898, was a final attempt to sway voters in the national plebiscite on Prohibition, taking place the next day. The "drys" won, but no changes came about as a result of the plebiscite.

Maritimes and rural areas of Ontario. Major cities, however, stayed wet, as did almost all of Quebec.

Liberal prime minister Sir Wilfrid Laurier raised the hopes of temperance agitators in 1895 by establishing a Royal Commission on the Liquor Traffic. But the commission recommended no changes to the status quo. Considering that liquor was an important source of revenue for the federal government, their recommendation is not surprising. How could a royal commission deny Ottawa its golden goose? From 1794, when the first still licence had been issued in Canada, until the mid-1800s, liquor was the government's single biggest source of income. Besides, the distilling industry had considerable power in Ottawa: Seagram, Corby, and Wiser were all

members of Parliament at one time or another. Under these circumstances, what were the chances that Canada would turn off the taps?

But the Prohibition issue wouldn't go away. In 1898, the whole country went to the polls for a national plebiscite on Prohibition. The question posed was, "Are you in favour of passing an Act prohibiting the importation, manufacture, or sale of spirits, wine, ale, cider and all other alcoholic liquors for use as a beverage?"

Sergeant Duncan Munn carries
out the Canada Temperance
Act in Moncton, 1907, as his
fellow officers look on.

Even though Prohibition won by 13,687 votes, or 52.5 per cent of the vote, Sir Wilfrid Laurier's government decided against passing a law. Only 44 per cent of voters had turned out — well below the usual turnout for elections. Furthermore, Quebec and British Columbia were dead set against Prohibition. Laurier's riding was in Quebec, along with many other Liberal seats. Temperance fighters must have felt considerable bitterness. Even though they had won the plebiscite, they had lost the battle. The issue was promptly dropped by Laurier's government.

The huge number of women behind the Prohibition movement, many of whom believed Prohibition would improve home and family life for Canadians, were let down. As yet without the vote, they had had to rely on men to vote in the Prohibition objectives. If women had been voting in 1898, the national plebiscite would have looked far more decisive and Canada's social history might have turned out quite differently.

Prohibition in Canada

Temperance fighters realized they were not going to get any help from Ottawa. The provinces began to take matters into their own hands. Between 1915 and 1917, every province voted in some degree of

March 9, 1916. Despite a snow storm, Ontario residents demonstrate for Prohibition at Queen's Park with fifteen thousand marchers, twenty bands, and three truckloads of petitions — one of them half a mile long!

The Dominion Alliance's Committee of One Hundred march to the Ontario legislature with 825 000 signatures for Prohibition.

Prohibition. (The qualifier is for Quebec, which prohibited spirits but not beer and wine.) In 1916, after an enormous demonstration at Queen's Park in Toronto that included fifteen thousand marchers, twenty bands, and three truckloads of petitions — one of them half a mile long — the Ontario government passed the Ontario Temperance Act. Bars and liquor stores throughout the province closed down. It was still quite legal to drink at home, however, and distilling, which was controlled by the federal government, continued throughout the province.

A year later, on March 11, 1918, the federal government finally took up the Prohibition cause, making the production, importation, and sale of all beverage alcohol illegal. The temperance fighters hadn't finally convinced Ottawa to see things their way; the government had merely enacted Prohibition as part of the War Measures Act. With young Canadian men fighting and dying in the trenches, somehow it didn't seem right to be drinking and having a good time at home. The country needed social discipline to win the war. Furthermore, the grain that was going into alcohol was needed for food production, and industrial alcohol was required for the war effort, mainly in synthetic rubber production. The distilleries turned their facilities over to producing industrial alcohol.

But even with full Prohibition, it was still possible to get a drink. Alcohol continued to be available for

Effective February 8, 1926

ONTARIO GOVERNMENT DISPENSARIES

Conducted Under Direction of

BOARD OF LICENSE COMMISSIONERS FOR ONTARIO

By Authority of

THE ONTARIO TEMPERANCE ACT

GENERAL PRICE LIST

Dispensaries sell liquor for medicinal, sacramental, scientific and manufacturing purposes only. The sale of liquor for beverage purposes in the Province of Ontario is prohibited by The Ontario Temperance Act.

DISPENSARIES:

No. 1 — 154 Wellington Street West, Toronto 2
No. 2 — 1271 Dundas Street West, Toronto 3
No. 3 — 29 Charles Street, Hamilton
No. 4 — 425 Talbot Street, London
No. 5 — 30 Sandwich Street West, Windsor
No. 6 — Market Street, Kingston
No. 7 — 92 Kent Street, Ottawa
No. 8 — 109 Simpson Street, Fort William

A. H. BIRMINGHAM

General Manager

154 Wellington St. West, Toronto 2, Ontario

Telephones: Elgin 5405-6-7

	Rep. Qt. R
1—Pol	$3.25

	p. Qt.	Litre Qt. R
	.60	
		$2.75
	2.25	
	1.00	
		2.25

SHERRY

	Imp. Qt.	Litre Qt. H
Gilbey Invalid	$2.00	
Molino		$2.25
Royal Palace		

The Ontario government ran several liquor dispensaries throughout the province for those in need of "medicinal" alcohol. Needless to say, the system was abused widely. (From The Seagram Museum Collection)

medicinal, scientific, mechanical, industrial, or sacramental purposes. Suddenly the number of heart conditions skyrocketed as patients showed up at government liquor dispensaries with doctors' prescriptions for rum or whisky. Stephen Leacock found the line-ups amusing: "It is necessary to go to a drug store and lean up against the counter and make a gurgling sigh like apoplexy," he wrote. "One often sees these apoplexy cases lined up four deep."[27]

The distillers lost no time responding to the new rules. Samuel and Harry Bronfman, for example, formed the Canada Pure Drug Company to market their "medicinal" alcohol. In Ontario, 810 thousand prescriptions were issued in 1923 and 1924. Reports have it that one doctor wrote 487 in a single day. Interns supported themselves by writing prescriptions: doctors received two to three dollars for each prescription they wrote. In British Columbia, one doctor ordered over four thousand bottles of alcohol in a one-month period before British Columbian doctors finally begged the government to take the "liquor trade" off their hands.

Federal Prohibition lapsed at the end of December 1919. Although the House of Commons voted to maintain Prohibition, the Senate, often referred to as the chamber of "sober, second thought," overturned the decision. Canadian distillers and brewers went back to business as usual. Prohibition was still alive and well, however, at the provincial level. All the provinces except Quebec retained their temperance legislation. The rest of the country's liquor stores and bars remained closed.

But those clever Canadian liquor producers found yet another loophole for getting their products to market, this time with the help of Canada Post. One might not be able to legally buy a bottle of whisky in Kingston or Peterborough, for example, but one could have it shipped in from Saskatchewan, or Quebec, or any other province where liquor was produced. For a thirty-month period, from 1920 until yet another plebiscite closed the loophole, many Canadian drinkers had their liquor delivered through the mail.

This advertisement from the *Daily British Whig* of 1916 shows what many Ontario liquor retailers did when the Ontario Temperance Act came into effect: they opened mail-order offices in other provinces.

This Hudson's Bay Company liquor store in Winnipeg, 1899, demonstrates just how creative store staff could be in displaying their merchandise before provincial governments took over.

After provincial governments took over in the 1920s, liquor stores became uninviting, institutional establishments like this one in Grimsby, Ontario.

Compromise: Provincial Liquor Control Boards

In the 1920s, the provinces finally found a moderate compromise: liquor control boards. From the governments' point of view, these provided a win-win situation. The federal government was seen to be doing something about the liquor traffic — controlling it — while the provincial governments now had their own golden goose. By 1930, every province had set up a system of provincially operated liquor stores except Prince Edward Island, which held out until 1948.

But even as they legalized alcohol, the provincial governments moved forward with uncertainty. Bars continued to be banned. Liquor stores were dark, uninviting establishments, and they were few in number. Liquor was kept hidden from view in storage rooms from which employees would retrieve bottles for the customers.

Regulations varied from one province to another, but most provinces kept records of who bought liquor, and how much. In Ontario, every customer had to purchase a two-dollar licence booklet, on which was kept a record of the amount of liquor they had bought. The system was a farce: if you lost your licence or forgot it, you simply bought another one. Manitoba's liquor records filled

An ironic outcome of Prohibition in North America was that women took up drinking.

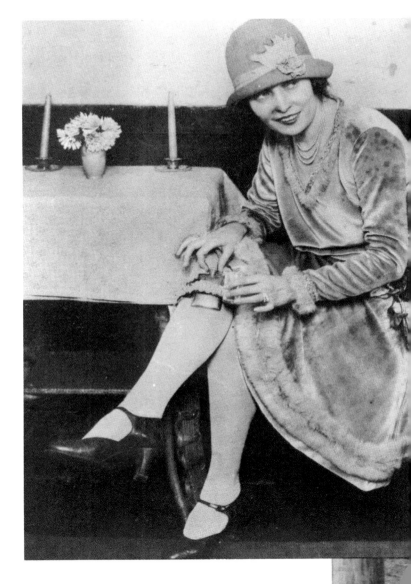

a huge warehouse, where dozens of clerks at desks entered licence records in ledgers that no one ever looked at. Eventually the booklets were replaced by a form on which customers had to fill in their name and address, then simply by a form on which they recorded the number of their purchases. Finally, in the 1960s, Ontario's liquor stores entered the modern age by eliminating the paperwork and bringing the liquor out front where customers could see what they were buying.

Even after the Liquor Control Act was passed, many communities voted not to have a liquor store. In Collingwood, for example, people refused to have one until 1938. Owen Sound was the last city in Ontario to go wet, which it did in 1972. The municipality of West Toronto — home of politician and temperance fighter William "Temperance Bill" Temple — remains dry to this day.

A raid on a "blind pig" — an illegal drinking establishment — in Elk Lake, Ontario

The Decline of the Temperance Movement

By the end of the 1920s, Canada's longest and strongest social movement was in decline. The provinces now controlled liquor distribution. Temperance advocates moved on to other issues such as women's suffrage. The exodus of people from the countryside into cities, and the immigration of large numbers of eastern European and Asiatic peoples to whom the concept of Prohibition was totally foreign, also contributed to the demise of the movement. Changing religious trends played a role as well. In the twentieth century, the number of Anglicans and Catholics grew while the Protestant fundamentalist religions that had promoted temperance slowed down. The union of the Methodist and United Churches further diluted the Methodist temperance message.

In 1927, the Ontario government introduced a new 375-mL bottle for spirits. Unlike its flask-shaped predecessor, this bottle was designed *not* to fit into a jacket pocket. (From The Seagram Museum Collection)

Did the Temperance Movement achieve its objectives? Drinking did decrease somewhat in Ontario and the Maritimes. But in western Canada, liquor consumption actually increased through the late 1800s and early 1900s. The Temperance Movement did provide the first real treatment for alcoholics, however, and probably brought about a reduction in the number of alcohol-related crimes. Interestingly, perhaps the most important legacy of the movement was the opportunity provided to Canadian women to begin moving beyond the realm of home and family and become involved in politics.

But while the Prohibition issue died in Canada in the 1920s, in the United States it was just heating up.

Ontario ended eleven years of province-wide Prohibition in 1927 with the opening of the province's first liquor store, in Toronto (above).

The decline in alcohol consumption that started in the late 1800s and continued until after World War Two was at least partly due to the Temperance Movement.

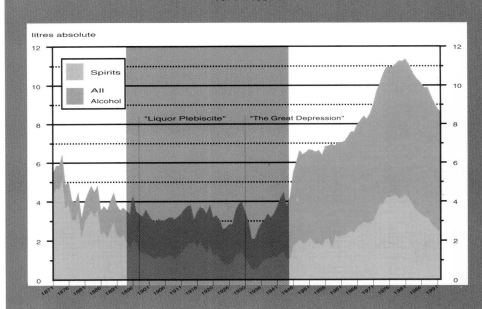

Canadian Per Capita Sales of Alcohol
1871 - 1991

litres absolute

Spirits

All Alcohol

"Liquor Plebiscite"   "The Great Depression"

With Prohibition in effect, illicit stills sprang up all over the country. This Edmonton operation, which could produce about two hundred gallons of moonshine whisky a week, was photographed for posterity before being seized by law enforcement officers.

Two members of the RCMP with a seized still, Carlyle, Saskatchewan, 1938

CHAPTER 6
Prohibition in the United States: The "Noble Experiment"

Four and twenty Yankees,
Feeling sort of spry,
Went across the border
To get a drink of rye.

When the keg was empty
The Yanks began to sing,
"God bless America",
But "God save the King!"

– *anonymous Prohibition Era song*[28]

Smuggled spirits made its way into the United States by the truckload and the boatload. Here, a speedboat leaves the mother ship, which is safely stationed in international waters, with a load of fifty cases of liquor.

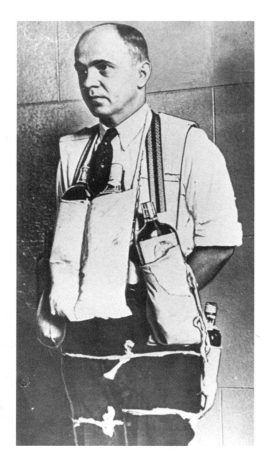  

While Canada flirted with Prohibition, the United States embraced it wholeheartedly. With the passing of the Volstead Act in 1920, the manufacture, sale, and transportation of all beer, wines, and spirits became illegal in the United States for the next thirteen years.

Prohibition may have been dubbed "the noble experiment" for Americans, but for Canadian distillers it was a dream come true. Suddenly there was a huge, thirsty market on their doorstep, with no competition from U.S. distillers. Certainly, drinking was illegal in the United States, but as long as they avoided selling directly to the American market, Canadian distillers and brewers weren't breaking any laws, at least not officially. Liquor flowed south like a river at dozens of points

Even law-abiding citizens found it hard to resist the temptation to make a few extra dollars on trips from Windsor to Detroit.

Police boats speed along the
St. Clair River between
Windsor and Detroit, a scene of
much smuggling during
American Prohibition.

R

LOADED OUTBOARD
SPEED BOAT

R WITH GLASS
ITING SIGNAL

along the Canada-U.S. border, and smuggling whisky, sometimes known nostalgically as "rum running," became a lucrative profession for an army of adventurous Canadians.

The smuggling trade was heaviest across Lakes Ontario and Erie in the early days of U.S. Prohibition. Hiram Walker, Wiser, Gooderham and Worts, and Corby were strategically located for this trade. Thousands of gallons of whisky crossed the lakes, most of it between Windsor and Detroit. Customs officials on both sides of the border turned a blind eye as men in rowboats, with official B-13 customs forms made out to exotic, far-off destinations such as the Bahamas or Cuba, left the docks at Windsor loaded to the gunwales with liquor only to show up a few hours later for another load.

Organized crime soon got wind of the large amounts of money being made, and gunfire became a nightly occurence on the St. Clair River, which separates Windsor and Detroit, as warring gangs staked out their territories. Ordinary citizens got involved, too, carrying contraband liquor in containers strapped to their bodies.

Once lookouts had determined that the coast was clear, smugglers on the St. Clair River could make the two-kilometre run in a matter of minutes. Only a fraction of the illicit cargos were stopped.

In western Canada, liquor was smuggled at several towns along the long undefended border between the Prairie provinces and the mid-western states. Much of the liquor came from the Bronfman brothers' plant in Yorkton, Saskatchewan. Smugglers removed the back seats of their cars, which allowed them to carry up to sixty cases. Lengths of chain dragging behind their cars and trucks turned up clouds of dust that made pursuit next to impossible. The town of Estevan, Saskatchewan, still celebrates its role in U.S. Prohibition with an annual Rumrunner's Festival.

People in southern British Columbia also got into the game, smuggling liquor to the states of California, Washington, and Oregon. In the early years of American Prohibition, boats were loaded in Vancouver or New Westminster and unloaded to smaller boats along the California coast. In 1922 and 1923, smugglers enjoyed smooth sailing. But by 1924, the U.S. Coast Guard was onto the West Coast activity. Over the next five years, many boats were seized. In 1929, however, smugglers began using a new route that included the transshipment port of Papeete, Tahiti. Papeete had warehouse facilities and authorities willing to co-operate with the smugglers.

Not all the liquor went south during Prohibition. This load of sixteen five-gallon cans of alcohol, confiscated at Hemmingford, Quebec, was being smuggled into Canada from the United States. It may have been homemade moonshine.

Smugglers load their cargo into a vessel at Windsor while an official looks on.

Liquor was smuggled in jute
sacks, which were lightweight,
rugged, and — unlike wooden
crates — would sink if thrown
overboard.

Loading Canadian Club at
St. Pierre's harbour

The Canadian Customs cruiser
Margaret plays "cat and mouse"
with a rum runner offshore.

As American and Canadian officials shut down the more easily managed border traffic, eastern smuggling operations soon needed a transshipment port as well. They found it in the French islands of St. Pierre and Miquelon, off southern Newfoundland. Canadian distillers and brewers could sell their products to French citizens, leaving the risky business of getting the liquor to its real market to the smugglers and American bootleggers.

Cleared on paper for destinations such as Cuba, the Bahamas, and Belize, the smugglers would head out to sea. Once in international waters, they would unload their cargo into small, fast launches that delivered it, usually in the dead of night, to points along the eastern seaboard between Boston and Atlantic City — the stretch known as "Rum Row." These small boats, often equipped with aircraft engines, could travel at up to thirty-five knots per hour, leaving the coast guard far behind. During the Prohibition Era, the government extended the three-mile limit off the east coast to twelve miles. This made control of the liquor trade somewhat easier. But even with this change, the U.S. Coast Guard was ill-equipped to handle the traffic and probably intercepted only 5 per cent of the liquor that traded hands.

Prohibition gave a boost to the ship-building industry on Canada's east coast. Shipyards that had been idle for years became active again, transforming fishing boats into rum

This "canned whisky" from Distillers Corporation— Seagrams Limited, produced approximately from 1929 to 1934, came in an unbreakable container. Was it a coincidence, or was this packaging developed for the illicit whisky trade? (From The Seagram Museum Collection)

runners. One of the most famous rum runners was *I'm Alone*, a two-masted schooner built at Lunenburg in 1924 and based in St. Pierre. This single ship was rumoured to have cleared $3 million worth of liquor in four years. Canada protested vigorously to the United States when the *I'm Alone* was sunk by the U.S. Coast Guard in 1929. One man drowned in this episode.

The French islands of St. Pierre and Miquelon had been involved in smuggling activities before and they are today, but never on the scale seen during U.S. Prohibition. By 1923, 500 thousand cases of liquor travelled through St. Pierre each year. Fishermen stopped fishing to turn to the more lucrative liquor trade as warehousemen and stevedores. Fishing boats were transformed into rum runners. Basements in private homes became storage facilities, and concrete warehouses sprang up overnight. More than a thousand vessels went through the tiny port in 1923 alone. The likes of it has never been seen in St. Pierre and Miquelon before or since.

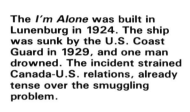

The *I'm Alone* was built in Lunenburg in 1924. The ship was sunk by the U.S. Coast Guard in 1929, and one man drowned. The incident strained Canada-U.S. relations, already tense over the smuggling problem.

This fish-processing plant on the French island of St. Pierre was converted into a giant liquor warehouse — with the liquor traffic being so lucrative, no one was fishing. Ships could load up right in front.

When a St. Pierre storekeeper told American gangster Al Capone that he liked his hat, Capone gave it to him. The straw skimmer is still on the island today, on display at the Hotel Robert Museum.

The French island of St. Pierre, off the south coast of Newfoundland, was a major transshipment point for liquor travelling from Canada to the United States. This photograph shows the St. Pierre harbour.

The End
of an Era

As American satirist Will Rogers put it, "Prohibition is better than no whisky at all." The Volstead Act was finally repealed on December 5, 1933. Nothing remains now but a set of amazing statistics that underline the bizarre nature of the era:

- By the end of the first year of U.S. Prohibition, there were twice as many "blind pigs" and "speakeasies" in the United States as there had been legal, licensed bars and taverns before Prohibition began.

- In 1925 alone, 4154 Americans died from drinking illegal moonshine.

- In 1931 the Canadian Coast Guard seized 2929 rum-running boats — an average of more than six boats a day.

- Revenues of the Canadian government from liquor export taxes increased by a factor of six during U.S. Prohibition.

North America's experiments with Prohibition had definitely changed attitudes towards alcohol. Perhaps it was a reaction to the rigid attitudes of the temperance agitators, or it may have been that "forbidden fruit tastes sweeter," as Ontario's temperance premier Ernest Drury once said, but once Prohibition was over, drinking was once again on the rise in North America. For one thing, during the 1920s and 1930s, it became acceptable for women to drink.

As far as the big distilleries were concerned, one can only wonder how their founders, Hiram Walker, Henry Corby, and Joseph Seagram, would have dealt with the Prohibition situation. All of them had died, however, before 1920. Certainly their sons were not comfortable with the new order, which required that distillers get involved in the underhanded work of developing a network of smugglers to deliver their goods — if their companies were to survive, that is. Times were changing, and the world in which the great barons of the Canadian whisky industry had built up their distilleries was fast disappearing. It took a different sort of entrepreneur to steer Canada's big distilleries through the Prohibition Era. The new generation, younger and more aggressive, had taken over the major companies during this time. Samuel and Harry Bronfman, through their Quebec distilling company, Distillers Corporation Limited, purchased Joseph E. Seagram & Sons in 1928, at the height of the Prohibition Era. A consortium of businessmen, including Herbert and Harry Hatch and L.J. McGuinness, bought Hiram Walker in 1926. Three years earlier they had also acquired Gooderham and Worts.

All of Canada's distillers supplied spirits to the U.S. market during Prohibition, though never directly. But when it was all over, they did admit to owing money to the U.S. government for import taxes not paid. Distillers Corporation–Seagrams Limited paid out $1.5 million. Other Canadian distillers made similar payments to the U.S. government.

The payments were not hard to come up with. The new owners of both Distillers Corporation–Seagrams Limited and Hiram Walker–Gooderham and Worts had made fortunes during Prohibition. Americans had developed a taste for Canadian whisky, and the Canadian industry still reaps the benefits sixty years later. Canadian distillers export 86 per cent of the whisky they manufacture in Canada to the United States. Canada's liquor industry is one of the largest in the world, and liquor is our sixth largest export. To a large extent, we have America's "noble experiment" to thank.

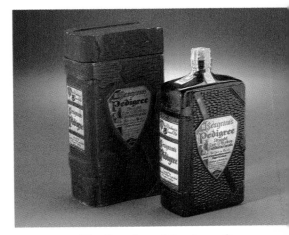

The Americans' fondness for straight rye whisky was satisfied with this product from Distillers Corporation–Seagrams Limited. (From The Seagram Museum Collection)

The Canadian distilling industry expanded from a production of eleven million litres of absolute alcohol in 1921 to forty-four million in 1929. This tremendous increase in output over just eight years was due partly to the end of Prohibition in Canada and the establishment of provincial liquor control boards, but far more to exports to the United States during U.S. Prohibition.

The stock market crash of 1929 and the depression that followed took its toll on the industry. In 1935, production of distilled spirits had gone back down to eleven million litres of absolute alcohol — a far cry from the peak reached in 1929.

With the outbreak of World War Two, distillers again turned their attention to making industrial alcohol and acetone for war purposes. All Canadian distilleries worked around the clock between 1941 and 1946, producing the high-proof industrial alcohol used in making smokeless powder, synthetic rubber, and pharmaceutical products. Some beverage

A Seagram's V.O. bottling line at the Waterloo distillery, 1948

alcohol continued to be made during the "distillers' holidays," which were days officially designated by the federal government as times when distillers could once again switch their plants over to beverage alcohol production. The amount placed in bond for maturing, however, declined drastically to seven million litres of absolute alcohol in 1943. Also, government regulations designed to conserve resources required that all

distillers bottle their spirits in "victory" bottles — plain, round bottles in fifths, pints, and half-pints.

At the end of the war, unaged spirits such as gin and liqueurs were available immediately. But whisky, with its ageing requirements, continued to be rationed because of limited stocks until the late 1940s. Until the early 1950s, liquor stores continued to limit the quantities that an individual could purchase of the most popular brands.

After the war, and with the Great Depression over, Canada entered a time of prosperity, and Canadian whisky sales boomed. The Temperance Movement was a thing of the past, and the cocktail era was in full swing. Whisky sours and Manhattans gave whisky an aura of sophistication it had never known before. As well, Americans continued their love affair with Canadian whisky. Its lightness had made it so popular with American drinkers that every major U.S. liquor distributor wanted to list Canadian whisky in its catalogues.

By the 1960s, sales of Canadian whisky were increasing by about 10 per cent each year. About this time, Canadian distillers began shipping whisky to the United States in bulk. New distilleries were built across Canada by Seagram, Walker, Gilbey, Schenley, and McGuiness to supply the West Coast and Far East markets. Production of Canadian whisky peaked in 1981 at nearly twenty-eight million litres of absolute alcohol.

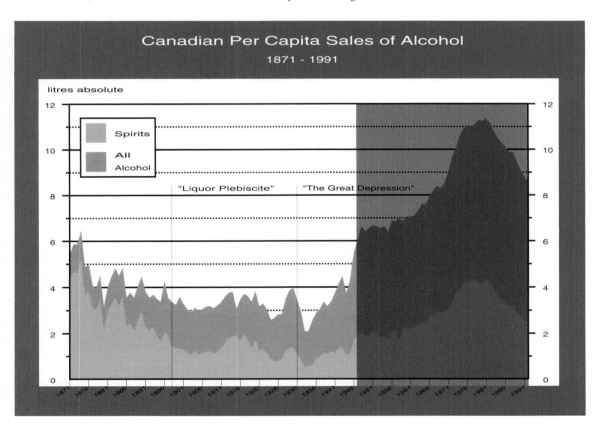

After World War Two, consumption of spirits increased, but liquor was never again to achieve the popularity of pioneer times. In marked contrast, Canadians began to drink beer and wine in record numbers.

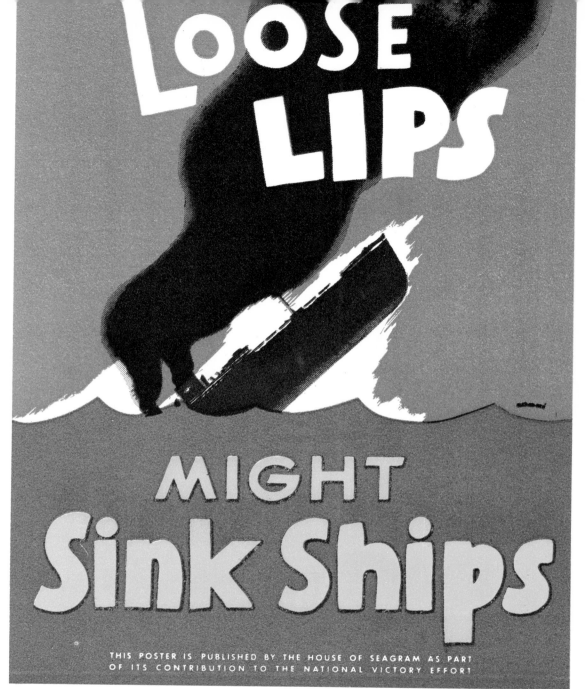

LOOSE LIPS MIGHT Sink Ships

THIS POSTER IS PUBLISHED BY THE HOUSE OF SEAGRAM AS PART OF ITS CONTRIBUTION TO THE NATIONAL VICTORY EFFORT

Forced once again to convert to industrial alcohol production during World War Two, distillers kept their names in the public's mind by sponsoring posters such as this one.

 **U**nder

New Ownership: Distillers Corporation– Seagrams Limited

During the postwar years, Seagram whiskies came to dominate the Canadian whisky industry worldwide. At the helm of this distilling empire was an energetic entrepreneur with a passion for good whisky: Samuel Bronfman.

The Bronfman family immigrated to Canada from Russia in 1889. They settled in Manitoba and, in 1903, purchased the Anglo American Hotel in Emerson, Manitoba. They acquired other hotels in Saskatchewan, Manitoba, and Ontario over the next few years, and soon the family of Abe, Harry, Samuel, and Allan and their brother-in-law Barney Aaron, prospered.

When provincial Prohibition laws forced them to close down the bars in their hotels, the Bronfmans imme-diately saw another business opportunity: the interprovincial mail-order liquor trade. They established a whisky blending facility in Yorkton, Saskatchewan, and began blending neutral spirits imported from the United States with Scotch whisky from Scotland. Their products were marketed to the United States and to Canadian customers via mail order.

In 1924, the Bronfmans formed Distillers Corporation Limited and built a large distillery in LaSalle, Quebec. Then, in 1928, they bought

The Bronfmans built their first distillery in La Salle, Quebec.

Joseph E. Seagram & Sons, changed their name to Distillers Corporation–Seagrams Limited (DC-SL), and became a public company. The same year, DC-SL entered into a fifty-fifty partnership with Distillers Company Limited (DCL) of Edinburgh, Scotland, then the largest distilling company in the world. The partnership gave DC-SL the exclusive right to produce and market world-famous DCL brands in Canada, rather than importing them from Scotland with the attendant duty and shipping charges.

Samuel Bronfman was convinced that U.S. Prohibition would not last long. He upgraded the distilleries at LaSalle and Waterloo with the best distilling equipment available, and built up personnel for the increased production and sales that Bronfman expected after repeal of the laws governing Prohibition. Bronfman's hunch turned out to be correct. The Volstead Act was voted out on December 5, 1933.

Samuel Bronfman (1889–1971). In recognition of his contributions to the whisky industry and to Canadian society, Samuel Bronfman was named a Companion of the Order of Canada in 1968.

DC-SL and DCL amicably parted company that year. DC-SL then moved into the U.S. market by purchasing distilleries south of the border. The first was in Lawrenceburg, Indiana, where the surrounding farmland provided high-quality corn, and the deep wells, a ready supply of pure, clean water. A state-of-the-art distillery was built in Louisville, Kentucky. During its opening week in 1937, over seventy thousand people visited the plant's thirteen buildings, directed by 125 uniformed guards. Seven thousand mint juleps were served.

Seagram's 7 Crown was launched for the U.S. market in 1934. The next year, the new brand passed the one-million-cases-a-year mark, becoming the best-selling spirit in the United States, a position it maintained for the next several years.

The move into the United States proved to be very profitable. By 1956, sales had risen to nearly $100 million. DC-SL moved into magnificent new U.S. headquarters designed by architect Mies van der Rohe, on Park Avenue in New York City in 1957. In 1958, the company was unquestionably the world's leading distiller.

Back home in Canada, Samuel Bronfman created a new whisky blend, Crown Royal, in honour of a visit from Queen Elizabeth and King George VI in 1939. Bottled in a crown-shaped bottle and dressed in a royal purple bag, Crown Royal became the epitome of Canadian whisky. The story goes that Bronfman tried out six hundred different blends before he finally settled on the one that was to become Crown Royal. The royal purple bag was a popular item, too. Few Canadian children in the 1940s and 1950s didn't keep a collection of marbles in a Crown Royal bag.

In 1942, Samuel Bronfman bought Henry Reifel's British Columbia Distillery Company Limited in order to build up stocks of aged whisky for the insatiable U.S. market. This included the Calvert distillery in Amherstburg, Ontario. Bronfman purchased United Distillers Limited in 1953 and created Thomas Adams Distillery, with its own new brands. Another distillery, Montmorency Distillery Ltd., at Beaupré, Quebec, was acquired in 1955.

Throughout the 1960s and 1970s, sales of Seagram whiskies continued to grow at an impressive pace. The company began more intensive marketing overseas, and acquired several more distilleries and wineries in North America and Europe.

Samuel Bronfman was as creative in marketing as he was in sales. Proud of the heritage of the Seagram company, he decorated the necks of V.O. bottles with elegant ribbon in black and gold, the racing colours of Joseph Seagram's winning thoroughbreds. At the peak of production, in the 1970s, Seagram used up sixteen thousand kilometres of this ribbon every year.

The Seagram Building in New York City, built in 1956–58, was designed by architects Mies van der Rohe and Philip Johnson. Photograph by Ezra Stoller, 1958. Courtesy Joseph E. Seagram & Sons, Inc.

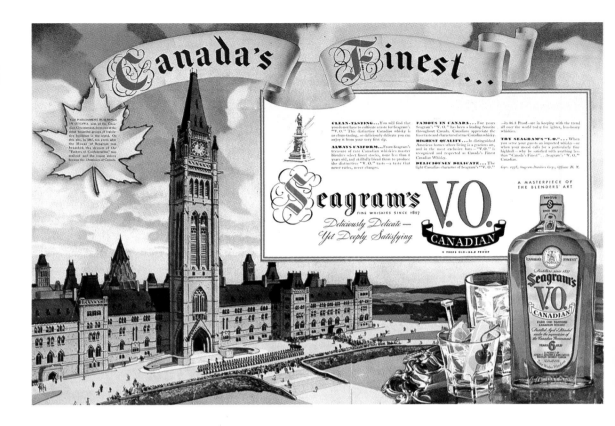

Bronfman also had enormous pride in his country and wanted to show it off to the world. He commissioned Canadian artists to do paintings of Canada's capital cities, and sent the show on an international tour, promoting Seagram's V.O. along with it. He also created a series of labels featuring Canada. It's interesting to look at these didactic labels today, to get another view of the ten provinces of Canada.

Another interesting and unusual marketing move was Bronfman's moderation campaign, which promoted drinking in moderation. This series of ads, begun in 1934, are still running today. So popular was this move that, all told, Samuel Bronfman received more than a hundred and fifty thousand letters of support and congratulations.

In 1968, at the age of seventy-seven, Samuel Bronfman received the highest Canadian civilian award: he was named a Companion of the Order of Canada. "Mr. Sam" as his employees affectionately called him, died in 1971. No other Canadian has influenced the distilling industry as deeply as Samuel Bronfman. His company, now known as The Seagram Company Ltd., is the only large multinational distiller to remain a Canadian company.

PROVINCE OF NOVA SCOTIA
ONE OF THE GREAT CANADIAN TEN

NOVA SCOTIA

Key to the North Atlantic. The thriving city of Halifax, Nova Scotia, is the key harbour of the North Atlantic. Hundreds of miles nearer Europe than New York or Montreal, its great harbour, Bedford Basin, welcomes and launches seagoing ships plying the trade routes of the world. Famous the world over for its fruit and seafood, Nova Scotia is populated by a hardy race of English and Scottish descent. Famous too for its natural beauty and charm, indeed, this province is truly one of the great "Canadian Ten."

CANADA SENDS HER BEST

CANADIAN
TEN
Canadian
Whisky

CHOICE WHISKY
SPECIALLY DISTILLED
AND MATURED TO PERFECTION
UNDER THE SUPERVISION OF THE
CANADIAN GOVERNMENT BY

CANADIAN DISTILLERS
LIMITED
MONTREAL   CANADA

QUEBEC   ONTARIO
BRITISH COLUMBIA   MANITOBA
SASKATCHEWAN   ALBERTA
NEW BRUNSWICK   NOVA SCOTIA
NEWFOUNDLAND   PRINCE EDWARD IS.

DIST NO 6   8   PORT 10 D

Anxious to tell the world about his beloved Canada, Samuel Bronfman oversaw the production of both ads and labels with Canadian content. The company also commissioned a series of paintings of Canadian cities, which then toured the world.

A Job for Life

Canada's major distilleries were good places to work, especially during the decades after World War Two, when sales boomed and the industry thrived.

Employees felt a fierce loyalty to the companies they worked for and took great pride in what they were doing. Many employees of Seagram, Hiram Walker, and the others devoted their whole careers to their companies. In return, the distilleries treated their employees well. A spirit of friendship and caring prevailed, not only within individual companies, but across the whole industry.

It was not unusual for employees to spend forty years or more with a company, moving through a variety of positions in production, administration, sales, marketing, and management. As a result, employees avoided stagnation in their work and became extremely valuable to the company because of their broad knowledge of various aspects of the industry. Many employees enjoyed the opportunity to work in different countries, which kept their jobs exciting and challenging.

Peter Melrose, who spent a long career with the Seagram company, remembers how employees worked together to develop innovative techniques and to improve productivity. "We were like one big family. Everyone in the industry was a friend to everyone else. We would go and visit the staff at Hiram Walker and Schenley to see how

they were doing things. Even after distillery employees retire, they continue to feel strong affec- tion for the company that they worked for, and for the industry as a whole." Now in his retire- ment, Melrose works part-time as an interpreter at The Seagram Museum in Waterloo, Ontario.[29]

Scenes from bottling departments at Hiram Walker

Harry Hatch

The Hatch Family and Hiram Walker–Gooderham and Worts

Harry Hatch was born in Ameliasburg, Ontario, in 1884. Like the Bronfmans, he entered the liquor business by purchasing a small hotel with a bar. Eventually he attained the position of sales manager at Corby. In 1923, Harry and his associates, who included his brother Herbert and distiller L.J. McGuinness, bought Gooderham and Worts. Three years later they purchased Hiram Walker, reorganizing their two companies as Hiram Walker–Gooderham and Worts. This ambitious consortium also started up the Canada Malting Company and later bought the Brights and Jordan wineries.

Like Samuel Bronfman, Harry Hatch speculated that the repeal of Prohibition would not be long in coming. He built up stocks of aged Canadian Club, and in 1933 moved into the U.S. market, building the world's biggest distillery in Peoria, Illinois. Hiram Walker continued to produce its popular Canadian Club, but it also introduced a new brand, called "Imperial," in 1941. Brands had come to be an important aspect of whisky marketing, as consumers tended to develop brand loyalties. Building up brands had been discontinued during Prohibition and World War Two, but it began again with a vengeance after the war.

Hiram Walker had always been a leader in the area of merchandising, and the company developed some innovative approaches in the early 1940s. For example, the company began gift-wrapping its liquor. This sounds like a fairly simple idea, but machinery to do the wrapping had to be designed, manufactured, and added to the standard bottling line. The concept began with a simple carton but eventually became more elaborate, with cartons being wrapped in foil paper with a ribbon and bow specifically designed for each brand. Over time, the entire spirits industry adopted the gift-wrap idea.

Hiram Walker also had great success with the "Adventure Series," magazine advertisements for Canadian Club. These ads, which appeared regularly in *Life* and many other magazines from 1934 until 1981, used a unique story-board approach. In six panels, the ads told the story of someone experiencing an adventure in a far-off part of the world and ending the day with their favourite whisky — Canadian Club, of course. The ads became a well-recognized trademark of the brand. The Adventure Series was discontinued when magazines became smaller in format and unsuitable for the story-board approach. The Adventure Series was one of the longest-running ad campaigns in North American history: forty-seven years!

Harry Hatch died in 1946. His successor, a stylish bachelor called Ross Corbit, was totally dedicated to the company. Sales increased greatly under his direction, and the company began to pursue international business more aggressively. Today, Canadian Club is sold in 155 countries. Corbit was followed as chief executive officer in 1969 by Clifford Hatch.

Of all the Canadian distilleries, only Hiram Walker still makes whisky at the original site developed by its founder in 1858. It is also one of a handful of distilleries in Canada that manufactures, ages, blends, and bottles its whisky all at one site. Their main product, Canadian Club, continues to be an ambassador for Canada throughout the world. Hiram Walker is currently owned by Allied-Lyons of Britain.

The Canadian Club "Adventure Series" ran for forty-seven years. It ended when magazines went to a smaller format, which no longer suited the series' "story-board" approach.

Harry Hatch purchased Hiram Walker & Sons in 1928 and amalgamated it to form Hiram Walker–Gooderham and Worts.

# Boom Times and New Distilleries

As Canadian whisky sales grew throughout the 1940s, 1950s, and 1960s, entrepreneurs built new distilleries all over Canada and existing companies built new plants. Seagram, for example, opened a new distillery in Gimli, Manitoba, in 1967. Hiram Walker doubled its production facilities at Walkerville in 1967. In 1971, it built the Okanagan Distillery in Winfield, British Columbia, to supply West Coast and Pacific Rim customers with Canadian Club.

Sending Canadian whisky to the United States in bulk, which began in the 1960s, became common practice. Bulk exports decreased shipping costs and import taxes by 20 to 25 per cent. Canadian whisky was lighter and more palatable than U.S. blended whiskies, and Americans soon discovered that, for the same price, Canadian whisky was better.

Gilbey Canada

A British firm of gin and Scotch distillers, Gilbey opened a distillery to produce Canadian whisky in Toronto in 1946. Its distillery specialized in bulk whisky sales to the United States and was very successful with its most popular brand, Black Velvet. Palliser Distillers Ltd. in Lethbridge, Alberta, produces Gilbey products as well as its own line of whiskies. Gilbey is owned by International Distillers & Vintners, which is owned in turn by Grand Metropolitan PLC, a British multinational firm.

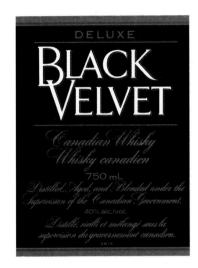

Canadian Schenley

Canadian Schenley was established at Valleyfield, Quebec, in 1945, as a subsidiary of the U.S. firm Schenley Distillers Corporation. The Canadian distillery's first export product was Canadian MacNaughton. In 1948 it introduced Golden Wedding to the domestic market, and then a year later, Canadian Tradition. In 1964 the plant underwent a major expansion and modernization and now employs two hundred people.

Schenley's Canadian whisky brands are Gibson's Finest, Gibson's Finest Sterling Edition, Golden Wedding, Canadian Schenley OFC (for Original Fine Canadian), Canadian Tradition, and Canadian MacNaughton. Schenley is owned today by the British firm Guinness as part of the United Distillers Group.

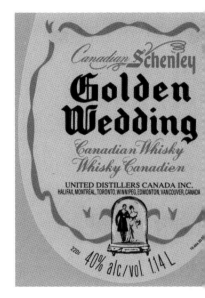

Alberta Distillers

Alberta Distillers was established in Calgary in 1946. Located in the heart of Alberta's rye-growing country, this company is the only distillery making Canadian whisky exclusively from rye grain. Rye is more expensive than corn, and it yields about one-third less starch. So why use only rye? Alberta Distillers believes that rye makes the best whisky. In its distilling, the company proudly uses

Canadian Mist

Canadian Mist Distillery was established in Collingwood, Ontario, in 1966 by the U.S. firm Barton Brands. The cold, clear water of Georgian Bay, adequate local supplies of corn, and the presence of grain storage elevators in Collingwood's harbour influenced their choice of location. In 1971, Barton sold the Canadian distillery to Brown-Forman Corporation, a family company from Louisville, Kentucky, founded in 1870.

Canadian Mist, a light, smooth, and mellow whisky with a trace of bourbon, travels in stainless steel tanker cars to Louisville for bottling and distribution. It is currently the number-one-selling Canadian whisky in the United States.

water from cold springs fed by Rocky Mountain glaciers, and it makes a point of ageing its whisky a thousand metres above sea level, in dry, pure, rarefied mountain air.

Alberta Distillers' Windsor Canadian was the first Canadian whisky to be shipped in bulk to the United States. It is placed third in current sales of Canadian whisky worldwide. Several other brands provide a wide range of whiskies, from the very light Alberta Premium to the heavier Alberta Springs Sipping Whisky.

Alberta Distillers is a subsidiary of the Jim Beam Brands Company, whose parent company is American Brands.

International Potter Distilling Corporation

International Potter was established in Vancouver in 1958 to serve the British Columbian market. Ernie Potter originally produced liqueurs from British Columbian–grown fruit. In 1962, British Columbian entrepreneur Harold Terry bought the business, and the company began making Potter's Special Old Canadian Whisky and Potter's Premium Vodka.

International Potter has a distilling division (Potter Distilling Company) with a plant in Kelowna, a wine division (Calona Wines), and a brewing division (Granville Island Brewing Co.). Potter's remains one of just a few independent distilleries left in the spirits industry.

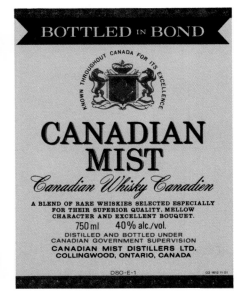

Many new distilleries were built across Canada from the 1940s to the 1960s. The Canadian Mist plant in Collingwood was built in 1966.

MELCHERS

VERY MILD®

Canadian Whisky Canadien

One of the Best
'Canadian'Whiskies of its Age
L'un des meilleurs whiskies canadiens
de son âge

MELCHERS INC. · MONTRÉAL · CANADA

750 mL 40% alc./vol.

D6P10D   4471K

Melchers

Melchers was established in the 1870s in Berthierville, Quebec, by Jan Melcher, a Dutch settler who made Geneva, or Dutch-style, gin. In 1928 Melchers was sold to the Marchand family, which upgraded the plant and began producing Canadian whisky. Like other Canadian distillers, the company grew rapidly in the 1960s, producing its own brands and blending and bottling Canadian whisky for other companies. Today, Melchers is owned by The Seagram Company Ltd.

CHAPTER 8
The Canadian Whisky Industry Today

The Canadian whisky industry has undergone major changes three times in its two-hundred-year history. The first was in the 1860s, when dozens of small distilleries closed down all over Upper and Lower Canada and a few major companies took over the industry. The second was during and after the U.S. Prohibition Era, when distillers consolidated to create large North American corporations and built fortunes in the U.S. market for Canadian whisky.

A third revolution is taking place today. Canadian whisky distilling companies are joining forces on a global scale with large multinational corporations, creating a complex web of shared ownership and international marketing arrangements. The days when one man or one family controlled a major distilling company in one country are long gone.

Four large, multinational corporations, one Canadian and three British, dominate the Canadian whisky industry today. While sales of Canadian whisky are down to 1960s' levels in North America, these four companies keep on doing very well, thanks to clever marketing strategies and diversification in the global marketplace.

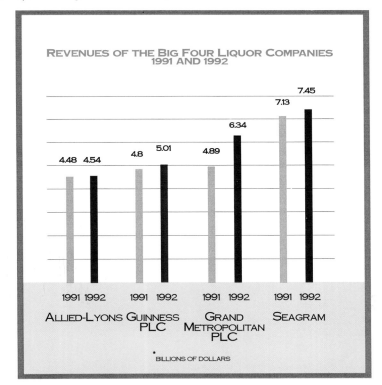

REVENUES OF THE BIG FOUR LIQUOR COMPANIES 1991 AND 1992

	Allied-Lyons		Guinness PLC		Grand Metropolitan PLC		Seagram	
	1991	1992	1991	1992	1991	1992	1991	1992
	4.48	4.54	4.8	5.01	4.89	6.34	7.13	7.45

* BILLIONS OF DOLLARS

Today's Canadian whisky industry is concentrated among four major players: three British and one Canadian.

113

The Seagram Company Ltd.

The Canadian-owned Seagram Company Ltd. is managed by the Bronfman family. The company has subsidiaries and affiliates in thirty countries. Besides Seagram's Canadian whiskies, the company also markets Chivas Scotch, Martell Cognac, and Mumm Champagnes. The Seagram company also manufactures and markets other spirits and wines, fruit juices, coolers, and mixers. The company also has a large financial interest in DuPont and Time Warner. In 1990, Seagram had sales of over $5 billion.

Since 1857 Depuis 1857

V.O. Light

CANADIAN WHISKY CANADIEN

*A fully-aged premium rye.
At least 30% fewer calories & 30% le[ss]
alcohol than full strength whisky.*

*Plus lé[ger] [c]alories e[t]
al[...]nte.*

750 m[L] % alc.

Seagram's
MUSEUM BLEND

CANADIA[N]
Blended and Bottle[d]

750 mL

Josep[h]
W[aterloo]

MUSEUM BLEND

This premium whisky is specially blended to commemorate the spirit of quality, tradition and craftsmanship of The Seagram Museum. All of the whiskies used in the blend were carefully distilled, aged and blended here in Waterloo, in Joseph E. Seagram & Sons 1857 original distillery adjacent to the museum building.

This unique whisky is sold exclusively at The Seagram Museum.

Cet excellent whisky est spécialement assemblé pour commémorer l'esprit de qualité, de tradition et de métier du Musée Seagram. Tous les whiskies qui entrent dans sa composition ont été soigneusement distillés, vieillis et assemblés ici à Waterloo, à la distillerie d'origine de Joseph E. Seagram & Fils fondée en 1857 et voisine du musée.

Ce whisky unique en son genre est vendu exclusivement au Musée Seagram.

Seagram's
FIVE STAR*
750 mL ★★★★★ 40% alc./vol.
RYE WHISKY

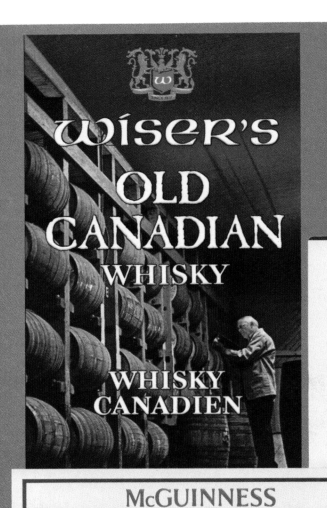

Allied-Lyons

Allied-Lyons, a British company, is a majority shareholder in the Hiram Walker Group, which also includes Gooderham and Worts, Corby, J.P. Wiser, McGuinness, James Barclay, Acadian Distillers, and Meagher's. Allied-Lyons also has interests in beer, wine, and food. In 1990 it had sales of over $5 billion.

PREMIUM

BY APPOINTMENT
TO THE LATE QUEEN VICTORIA ·1898·1901
TO THE LATE KING EDWARD VII·1901·1910

BY APPOINTMENT
TO THE LATE KING GEORGE V ·1910·1936
TO THE LATE KING GEORGE VI·1936·1952

Canadian Club

Canadian Whisky Canadien

C.C.

Distilled and Bottled under
adian Government Supervision by

M WALKER & SONS, LIMITED

Walkerville, Ontario, Canada.

Bottled in Bond

750 mL
40% alc./vol.

McGUINNESS
SILK TASSEL ®
Light

27% alc./vol.	CANADIAN WHISKY CANADIEN	48 Cal (201 kj)
750 mL	AT LEAST 30% FEWER CALORIES AND 30% LESS ALCOHOL THAN SILK TASSEL.	/30 mL
DIP57E	PLUS LÉGER D'AU MOINS 30% EN CALORIES ET EN ALCOOL QUE SILK TASSEL.	

NL-503

OLD CANADA   OLD CANADA   OLD CANADA

IMPORTED

CANADIEN

RR
ROYAL
RESERVE
CANADIAN RYE WHISKY

CORBY
WHISKY CANADIEN

BOTTLED UNDER GOVERNMENT SUPERVISION
TEILLÉ SOUS-LA SURVEILLANCE DU GOUVERNEMENT
EO · LES DISTILLERIES CORBY LIMITÉE, CORBYVILLE, ONTARIO, CANADA

50 mL – 40% alc./vol.

ESTʼD 1858
HIRAM WALKER'S
Northern
Light
CANADIAN
Blended Canadian

DISTILLED, AGED AND BLENDED
UNDER CANADIAN GOVERNMENT SUPE
40% ALC./VOL. (80 PROOF) PRODUCT
IMPORTED IN BOTTLE BY BARTON
CHICAGO, ILLINOIS.

D1-P57-E

MEAGHERS
1878
Canadian
Rye Whisky
Canadien

LA DISTILLERIE MEAGHER LTÉE · MEAGHERS DISTILLERY LTD.

750 mL RETURN FOR REFUND WHERE APPLICABLE · CONSIGNE LA OÙ LA LOI LE PRESCRIT 40% alc./vol.

AGED IN OAK · VIEILLI DANS LE CHÊNE

117

Grand Metropolitan

This British company owns Gilbey, the makers of Black Velvet Canadian whisky. They are also involved in food, wine, and retailing. In 1990, Grand Metropolitan's sales reached $9 billion.

Guinness

Guinness, another British company, is famous for its dark stout beer and the Guinness *Book of World Records*, produced by its publishing company. Mainly a brewing and spirits enterprise, Guinness owns United Distillers, which makes Canadian Schenley products: Gibson's Finest, Gibson's Finest Sterling Edition, Golden Wedding, Canadian Schenley OFC, Canadian Tradition, and Canadian MacNaughton. In 1990, Guiness's sales topped $5 billion.

The Economic Role of the Distilling Industry in Canada

Although in a period of decline, the Canadian whisky distilling industry still contributes greatly to the Canadian economy. The industry directly employed over six thousand Canadians at its peak in 1973. Since then, distilleries have closed down across the country. About forty-three hundred people have jobs in the industry today. Another twenty thousand are indirectly employed through regulation, distribution, and sales. The agriculture, manufacturing, distribution, transportation, tourism, and hospitality industries all benefit from Canada's distilling industry.

Canadian whisky is Canada's biggest-selling beverage alcohol export. In 1992, export sales reached $500 million, most of it going to the United States. Two generations after the Prohibition Era, Canadian whisky is still very popular with Americans, and Canadian whisky exports help to balance Canada's trade with the United States. In recent years, other markets, especially in the Pacific Rim countries, are becoming increasingly important. The industry sees potential for new markets in China.

Canadian whisky and other distilled spirits continue to be an important source of government revenue. In 1991, $3.4 billion worth of spirits (domestic and imported) were sold in Canada. These sales generated federal and provincial government revenues of about $2.5 billion. Excise taxes on spirits have increased from $6.237 per litre of absolute alcohol in 1975, to $11.066 in 1991. By raising the taxes, the government maintains its level of revenue from spirits, even though domestic sales are down.

The decline in sales has hit the distilling industry hard. Since 1981, sixteen distilled spirits plants across Canada have closed and forty-two hundred Canadians have lost their jobs. The Association of Canadian Distillers (ACD) maintains that sharp increases in the taxes on spirits are the major factor in declining spirits sales. Distilled beverages are taxed by the federal government at a rate 2.5 times higher than wine and twice as high as beer, even when all three types of alcoholic beverages are compared in terms of alcoholic content. These figures become even more inequitable after provincial markups

The Association of Canadian Distillers ran this ad in a major Canadian newspaper in early 1994.

International sales trainees
at Hiram Walker

FEDERAL EXCISE LEVIES* IN $/L.A.A.

YEAR	SPIRITS	BEER	WINE
1975	$6.237	$1.848	$1.008
1980	6.583	2.376	2.292
1981	6.805	2.450	2.362
1981	7.392	2.661	2.570
1982	8.514	3.066	2.957
1983	9.649	3.474	3.351
1984	10.120	3.642	3.513
1985	10.320	3.716	3.583
1986	10.733	3.865	3.727
1991	11.066	5.597	4.268

*In the Federal Excise Act, Excise Levies for beer are $/HL (dollars per Hectolitre) and for wine are $/L (dollars per Litre). For ease of Excise Rate comparison between the three alcohol beverages, the ACD has converted the rates for beer to $/L.A.A. (Litre of Absolute Alcohol) at 5% alcohol and for wine to $/L.A.A. at 12% alcohol.

Comparative excise rates for beer, wine, and spirits, 1975 to 1991

are applied. In Ontario, for example, the markup on spirits is 138 per cent of the landed cost, while for Ontario wine it is only 34.4 per cent and for beer it is fifty cents per litre or 21 per cent of the landed cost, whichever is more.

The ACD regularly lobbies the federal government to level the playing field with regard to federal taxes on beer, wine, and whisky. Until beverage alcohol products are taxed more fairly, the ACD is certain that the spirits industry will continue to suffer its long-term decline. Distilleries will continue to close, jobs will be lost, and businesses in related industries, from glass bottle manufacturers to hotels and restaurants, will suffer.

Although in a period of decline, the distilling industry still contributes greatly to the Canadian economy. The industry employs about forty-three hundred people directly, and as many as twenty thousand more indirectly, through spin-off industries.

The ACD also argues that the exorbitant price of spirits in Canada compared with that in the United States makes smuggling all too attractive. It estimates that as much as 25 per cent of the distilled beverages being consumed in Canada today are coming into the country, mostly illegally, from the United States. These big-time operations involve tanker-truckloads of contraband liquor. This situation costs Canada about $1 billion a year in lost jobs, economic activity, and taxes.

If Hiram Walker and Joseph E. Seagram were alive today, they would probably sympathize with the difficulties Canadian distillers must overcome. Walker and Seagram also coped with declining sales, economic recession, and dramatic increases in taxes on their product. On top of it all they had the Temperance Movement to deal with as well. In the past few centuries, Canada's whisky distillers have experienced everything from complete Prohibition to decades when sales grew 10 per cent per year. What the future will hold is anyone's guess.

Bottle-making plant in southern Ontario

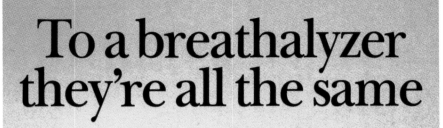

To a breathalyzer they're all the same

These standard servings of beer, wine and spirits all contain an equal amount of alcohol.

So don't be misled by appearances. And never mix drinking with driving.

DIFFERENT. BUT EQUAL.

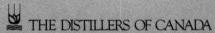
THE DISTILLERS OF CANADA

90 Sparks St., Suite 1100, Ottawa, Ont. K1P 5T8

The Association of Canadian Distillers has launched an "equivalency" campaign in the print media, informing readers that all alcoholic beverages must be drunk in moderation, and that a 5-ounce glass of wine at 12 per cent alcohol, a 12-ounce bottle of beer at 5 per cent alcohol, and 1.5 ounces of spirits at 40 per cent alcohol (the maximum found in a drink) all have the same alcohol content: 0.6 ounces.

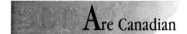 **A**re Canadian

Laws Fair to Distillers?

Besides the taxation issue, other inequities exist among the three groups of alcoholic beverage producers. One involves distribution.

On the one hand, in most of the provinces, spirits can be purchased only at liquor stores. Wine, on the other hand, is sold at wineries and through wine boutiques, as well as at provincial liquor stores. Beer can be sold at the breweries, through the Brewers' Retail chain, and — in some cases — at baseball games and other events. Even at the liquor stores, merchandising methods tend to promote wine over spirits.

Another inequity involves access to advertising. Beer and wine producers can advertise through broadcast media such as television and

Today Canadian distilleries are operating at 50 per cent capacity.

radio. Federal legislation, however, prohibits the use of the airwaves for advertising spirits. Even when it wanted to run ads against drinking and driving, the spirits industry was not granted air time.

 # Changing

Drinking Trends in Canada

Ninteenth-century temperance fighter Letitia Youmans would be happy with today's drinking trends. From 1981, when consumption of alcoholic beverages peaked in Canada, until 1992, consumption appears to have dropped sharply. The story with spirits is particularly dramatic: between 1981 and 1992, legal domestic spirits sales decreased by 46 per cent. Canadian whisky sales declined by more than half, from seventy-eight million litres to thirty-six million litres. Canadians are obviously changing their drinking patterns. What forces are bringing about these changes?

The most recent recession, like the one that plagued distillers in the late 1800s, has certainly played a role.

In recent years, the apparent consumption of alcoholic beverages has dropped in Canada.

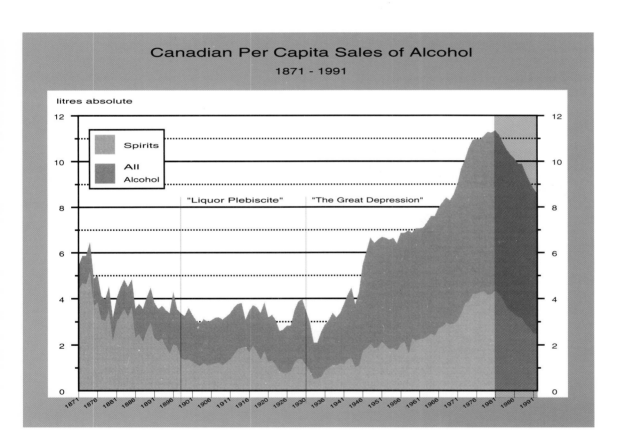

Unemployment is high; with less ready cash, consumers either drink less or obtain their alcoholic beverages by less expensive means, such as making or buying homemade beer and wine and smuggling liquor. (The decline in drinking, incidentally, does not take these factors into account.)

Interestingly, beer sales have dropped only slightly, and wine sales have actually increased, prompting one to think that lifestyle choices play an important role in the sales figures. Distillers have responded to the current interest in health by introducing new "light" spirits with a lower percentage of alcohol, but with little real success. They have done better with spirit-based "coolers" — another low-alcohol product. Among alcoholic beverages, wine is definitely the most in vogue in the 1990s. Sales have been buoyed by recent reports that wine in moderation is good for the health. Improvements in Canadian wines and the Canadian wine industry's vigorous efforts to market its product are also giving the industry a boost.

A final factor contributing to a decrease in alcohol consumption is the general ageing of the Canadian population. Older people tend to drink less, and many have less disposable income to spend on alcohol.

Is there any way of knowing which of these many factors is contributing most to the decline in whisky sales? Yes. Just ask how the situation in the United States compares with that in Canada. South of the

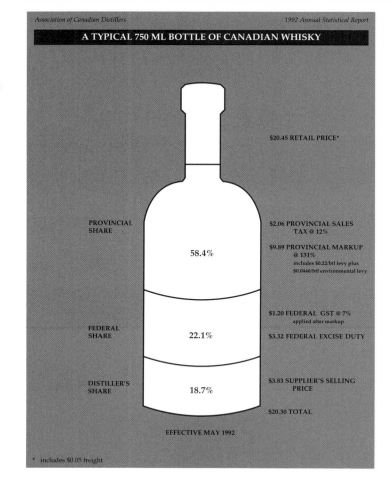

A TYPICAL 750 ML BOTTLE OF CANADIAN WHISKY

$20.45 RETAIL PRICE*

PROVINCIAL SHARE

58.4%

$2.06 PROVINCIAL SALES TAX @ 12%

$9.89 PROVINCIAL MARKUP @ 131%
includes $0.22/btl levy plus $0.0446/btl environmental levy

FEDERAL SHARE

22.1%

$1.20 FEDERAL GST @ 7%
applied after markup

$3.32 FEDERAL EXCISE DUTY

DISTILLER'S SHARE

18.7%

$3.83 SUPPLIER'S SELLING PRICE

$20.30 TOTAL

EFFECTIVE MAY 1992

*   includes $0.05 freight

forty-ninth parallel, the apparent decline in consumption of spirits is about half what it is in Canada. The U.S. lifestyle (emphasis on fitness, health, etc.) is fairly similar to that in Canada, as is the general economic outlook. But taxes on spirits are far lower than they are in Canada. These facts would appear to indicate that taxes and the resulting high prices of spirits could be responsible for about 50 per cent of the decline in spirits consumption in Canada.

CHAPTER 9
The Art and Science of Canadian Whisky

 **W**hat Goes

Into Canadian Whisky?

The Grains

Corn, rye, and barley are the grains that go into Canadian whisky. Corn is used for the base whisky. Rye and barley produce the flavouring whiskies that the distiller blends with the base whisky. Barley also provides malt, which contains enzymes essential to the whisky-making process.

Corn

One of the most versatile of the world's grains, and the only one that originated in the Americas, corn is the staple food of more than two hundred million people in eighteen countries in Latin America and Africa. Industry uses corn in an endless array of non-food products such as paper, paint, plastic, and soap. It also happens to serve as the principal ingredient of whisky in both the United States and Canada.

Any grain could be used to produce the highly refined, almost pure base whisky that makes up about 85 per cent of Canadian whisky, but most distillers use corn. The reason is economic: of all the grains, corn yields the largest amount of starch. The corn selected must pass rigorous quality control tests before going into Canadian whisky. It must be sweet and ripe, with few damaged kernels. It must be dried to a moisture content of 14 per cent. Corn

During the 1950s and 1960s, the Seagram company collaborated with scientists to develop new strains of cold-tolerant corn that would grow in Manitoba.

that has a higher moisture content could become mouldy in storage, and mouldy corn would produce a whisky with an unacceptable musty flavour.

Until the 1960s, not much field corn was grown in Canada outside Essex and Kent Counties in southwestern Ontario. Canadian distillers imported their corn from the United States. Even today, during years such as 1992, when the cool, wet summer reduced the quantity and quality of yields, distillers still import corn from the United States. But that is unusual. Today, with corn grown in every province except Newfoundland, especially in Ontario, Quebec and Manitoba, Canadian distillers rely mainly on Canadian corn for their products.

The Seagram company has played an important role in increasing the amount of Canadian corn that goes into Canadian whisky. In 1962 the company adopted a Canadian-corn purchasing policy and initiated a program to stimulate corn production in Canada, especially in areas where the crop could be grown but wasn't. With its plans to build a new distillery at Gimli, Seagram was particularly interested in growing corn in Manitoba. At that time, existing corn varieties could not be grown with any degree of certainty in Manitoba because of the province's cool climate and short growing season.

Seagram scientists collaborated with scientists at the University of Manitoba to create new hybrids that would grow in that province. Manitoba corn was crossed with corn that had been grown in harsh conditions high in the Andes Mountains of Peru. The resulting cold-tolerant hybrids thrived in Manitoba. The team undertook extensive testing to evaluate the quality and yield of whiskies produced with the new hybrids. Today, thanks to scientists at the University of Manitoba and to Seagram, which funded a corn research chair at the University, waving fields of corn reach to the sun in Manitoba, and Canadian corn goes into the whiskies made at Gimli.

Rye

Once the predominant bread grain for the poor of northern Europe, rye was brought to North America by Europeans. Originally, rye was viewed as a weed that competed with wheat and reduced yields. Closely related to wheat, it can interbreed with it. But rye's drought- and disease-resistance, along with its ability to grow in impoverished soils and acidic conditions, gave it commercial importance in northern Europe centuries ago.

Today, rye ranks seventh among

An Alberta Distillers employee takes a sample of rye as the grain is unloaded at the Calgary distillery.

the world's food and feed crops. Winter rye, which farmers sow in the fall, is the type usually grown. Most of Canada's rye is grown for export. About 30 per cent feeds livestock, and roughly 13 per cent goes to the distilleries.

Although Canadian whisky is often called "rye," this nickname is a bit of a misnomer, because the principal ingredient of Canadian whisky is corn. But rye remains one of the most important grains in determining the taste of Canadian whisky. With its spicy flavour and scent, detectable even in the dried grain,

rye is used in whisky making as seasoning is used in cooking.

Perhaps only one Canadian whisky producer can truly call its product "rye." Alberta Distillers, as mentioned in chapter 8, makes both its flavouring and base whiskies from 100 per cent rye grain. Each year it buys two million bushels of rye, worth over $1.7 million, from seven hundred Alberta farmers, many of whom have been supplying the distillery for two generations. Although the company produces less than 10 per cent of Canada's whisky, it uses 75 per cent of the rye grain used by

distillers in Canada. Rye is more expensive than corn, and it yields less starch. Yet Alberta Distillers believes that rye simply makes the best whisky.

Like barley, rye can also be malted, or germinated, and used for its starch-converting enzymes. Rye malt, however, produces a differently flavoured whisky than barley malt does.

Rye, the grain that gives Canadian whisky its unique flavour, is a cold-weather crop that grows in many regions of the country.

Barley

Highly adaptable and easily grown, barley was among the earliest cultivated crops. It served as the chief grain of Europe until the sixteenth century. Today, about half of all the barley grown in the world goes into livestock feed; much of the rest goes into beer and whisky making. In Canada, barley grows best in the Prairie provinces, where it is sown in spring.

In both brewing and distilling, barley plays a crucial role. Although raw barley is used, like rye, as a flavouring element, barley serves, more importantly, as the source of malt, which provides the enzymes that convert plant starch into sugar.

When barley grains germinate, they produce enzymes known collectively as "diastase." Diastase turns the starch in the grain into sugar, making it available as a food source for the embry-

onic plant. Diastase does the same thing for the distiller. Once the starch in the mash has been converted to smaller sugar molecules, the yeast can go to work on it, turning it into alcohol and carbon dioxide through the action of another group of enzymes that come from the yeast cells. (Enzymes are catalysts, speeding up chemical reactions.)

Any grain can be used as malt, but barley outdoes all others in its ability

At its tower malt house in Calgary, Canada Malting turns barley grown in the Prairie provinces into high-quality malt for distillers and brewers.

to convert starch to sugar: one part of barley malt can convert two thousand parts of starch in any grain into fermentable sugar.

To make malt, the maltster soaks the grains, allowing them to germinate. As the embryonic plant begins to develop, the grain produces more and more enzyme, until no more is necessary to saccharify, or turn into sugar, all the starch available in the kernel. At this point, which occurs within a few days under optimum conditions, the grains are kiln-dried to arrest development. Timing is critical for the maltster. If he or she allows the tiny germinating plants to break through the skin of the grains, the point of maximum enzyme production has been missed.

The dried barley, now known as malt, is ground into a powder for use by distillers, brewers, and food processing companies. In recent years, distillers have begun using natural enzymes produced by fungi as well; this allows them to make the conversion from starch to sugar more complete.

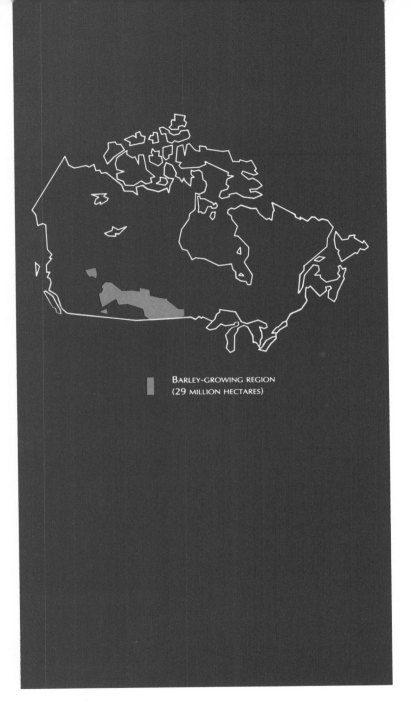

BARLEY-GROWING REGION
(29 MILLION HECTARES)

In the Prairie provinces, nearly thirty million hectares of barley yield over eight million tonnes of the grain each year. Canada Malting Company, the largest malt-producing organization in the world, selects five hundred thousand tonnes of the choicest barley to produce malt for brewers, distillers, and the food industry.

131

Yeast: The Workhorse of the Distilling Industry

Without yeast, a tiny one-celled plant, we could not make beer, wine, or spirits. As well as being the organism that actually makes the alcohol, yeast also determines — to a large extent — the flavour of the final product. In whisky making, yeast interacts with the grain mash and the water to create subtly different whiskies. Using the same basic ingredients, a distiller can use one yeast to produce a whisky with a grape flavour, and use another yeast to give the whisky a peachy taste. Whiskies made with different yeasts can also be blended to achieve a particular final product.

When choosing yeasts, distillers look for good flavour characteristics, rapid growth, efficient conversion of sugar to alcohol, resistance to changes in temperature and acidity, and the ability to work in mixtures with high concentrations of sugar and alcohol. Distillers maintain "libraries" of hundreds of different yeast cultures, and guard their best strains carefully. Hiram Walker's distillery today makes its Canadian Club whisky with yeast descended from the strain Walker himself began using in the 1870s.

Yeast at work. This one-celled organism has been called "the workhorse of the distilling industry."

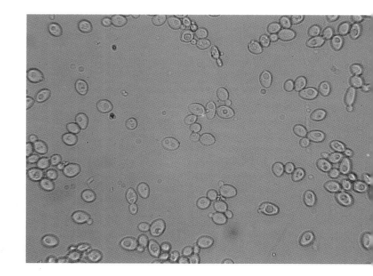

Yeast is used to make all fermented and distilled beverages. Many of these yeast cells are producing new offspring through the process of budding.

The Water in Whisky

A reliable source of pure water is one of the most important prerequisites for making "the water of life." The production process uses water extensively, for both mashing and cooling. An important ingredient of whisky, demineralized water tops off the final aged and blended product to ensure the proper strength of alcohol. The water used in all these stages has a definite influence on the taste of whisky.

The water that goes into whisky must be pure; foreign elements can adversely affect the flavour. It should contain natural salts and minerals in the right proportions. The Canadian Mist plant in Collingwood draws on the clear, alkaline waters of Georgian Bay for its whisky. The Seagram plant at Gimli, Manitoba, gets its process water from two wells fed by an aquifer lying between rock layers that run from Lake Winnipeg to Lake Manitoba. This water is hard, with levels of calcium and other minerals that make it very desirable for manufacturing the various whisky distillates produced at Gimli. Palliser Distillery of Lethbridge and Alberta Distillers of Calgary draw their water from rivers fed by Rocky Mountain glaciers. Quite appropriately, the word *calgary* means "clear running water" in Gaelic.

The Seagram plant in Gimli, Manitoba, with Lake Winnipeg in the background. Clean air and clean water were two of the factors that led the Seagram company to establish a new distillery at this site in 1967.

The 1950s and 1960s: Decades of Experimentation at Seagram

During the 1950s and 1960s, Seagram conducted extensive research into all aspects of the whisky-making process. Laboratory scientists tried out dozens of rye and barley hybrids, from a wide variety of locations. They developed a new hybrid rye, giving it the name "Rosner" — the maiden name of Samuel Bronfman's wife. The scientists studied new mashes of wheat and oats. They even tried buckwheat, in the production of bourbon. (Food and Drug regulations allowed for bourbon production in Canada until the 1950s.)

The products to emerge from all this experimentation were described as, among other things, "distinctive," "unique," and "dry, with an estery fruity flavour." Some of the new mash bills produced superior quality whisky and so were put to good use. Others failed to improve on the quality of Seagram whiskies and were abandoned.

Seagram scientists also experimented with malt. They found that various malts had different diastatic powers (the power of the enzyme reaction), but the effect on flavour was not as strong as the effects of other factors, such as type of barrel and location of maturing warehouse. The scientists also collected and experimented with hundreds of different yeast strains. They discovered five new strains that Seagram still uses today.

Two experiments were conducted with barrels. One was a sort of cradle, in which the barrels were continually rocked. The idea was to imitate the motion of a boat. People first realized that whisky improved with age back in the days of sailing ships: some observant drinkers noted that whisky tasted smoother after it spent a few months crossing the Atlantic in oak barrels. This experiment did in fact speed up the maturing process, but the cost of continuously rocking thousands of barrels ruled out any chance of implementation.

The other barrel experiment — a square whisky barrel — can be seen on display at The Seagram Museum in Waterloo. Ageing whisky in a square barrel did seem to result in a whisky of a different character, but the logistics of moving square barrels soon proved this experiment a dud.

One of Seagram's experiments was the square barrel. Although the whisky that aged in it did show some unique characteristics, the idea was soon abandoned because the barrels were too difficult to move around. (From The Seagram Museum Collection)

134

**Changing screens in the
hammer mills at Hiram Walker**

Is Made

Milling and Mashing

To begin with, all the grains are cleaned and stored in tall bins. When needed, the grain is milled to expose the starch. Three different types of mills help achieve the desired size and uniformity of particles. The meal is weighed and conveyed to the mash tun — a large cooking vessel with agitators that thoroughly mix the meal with water. As the mixture is cooked with steam, it becomes starchy or gelatinized. In this state, the starch converts easily into sugar by the addition of malt and other enzyme sources. This complex chemical process, called mashing, takes place over a few hours, at temperatures ranging from 63° C to 100° C, depending on the type of whisky being made. In some operations, mashing takes place continuously, under pressure, while in others, it is done at normal atmospheric pressure, in batches.

Mashes made with more than one grain are combined in the proportion required for the type of whisky being made. A mash bill of 98 per cent corn and 2 per cent barley malt, for example, will produce a very light whisky with corn as the predominant flavour element. A mash bill of 90 per cent rye and 10 per cent barley malt will yield a flavourful whisky with typical rye character.

Fermentation

Machines pump the mash mixture into large stainless steel fermentation tanks, where the yeast will work its magic, converting the sugar in the grain to alcohol and carbon dioxide. The fermentation process in whisky making is similar to the process used to make beer and wine. Confusing matters, the fermented whisky mash is called "beer."

Like malt, yeast works through the action of enzymes. The chemical process is straightforward:

$$C_6H_{12}O_6 + \text{enzyme action} = 2C_2H_5OH + 2CO_2$$

During fermentation, the yeast multiplies as it feeds on the sugar. The distiller must keep everything absolutely sterile at this stage. Bacteria or moulds could suppress yeast growth and produce a poor-quality whisky. For fermentation, the mixture should be kept between 18° C and 32° C. Unwanted organisms that create undesirable flavours would appear at temperatures above 32° C.

As the yeasts multiply, the mash seethes and foams. When the seething subsides, the mash, now known as beer, goes to the beer still for distillation. The beer contains alcohol as well as other compounds known as esters, aldehydes, and fusel oils that form in side reactions during the fermentation process. These compounds, called "congeners," give whisky its flavour.

How Does a Hydrometer Work?

Everyone involved in the production of alcohol, from home wine makers to industrial distillers, uses a hydrometer to measure alcohol. A hydrometer indicates the relative density, or specific gravity, of a liquid (which compares the density of the liquid with that of water). The specific gravity of water is 1.000. Alcohols have a lower specific gravity than water (e.g., 0.992) while whisky mash or crushed grapes have a higher specific gravity (e.g., 1.082).

The hydrometer is graduated, with higher numbers at the bottom and lower numbers at the top. In the early stages of fermentation, when the sugar content of the mixture is still high, the hydrometer floats high, giving a specific gravity of greater than 1.000. When the yeast has converted most of the sugar to alcohol, the liquid is less dense and the hydrometer sinks lower, giving a specific gravity reading of less than 1.000.

The yeast room at Hiram Walker

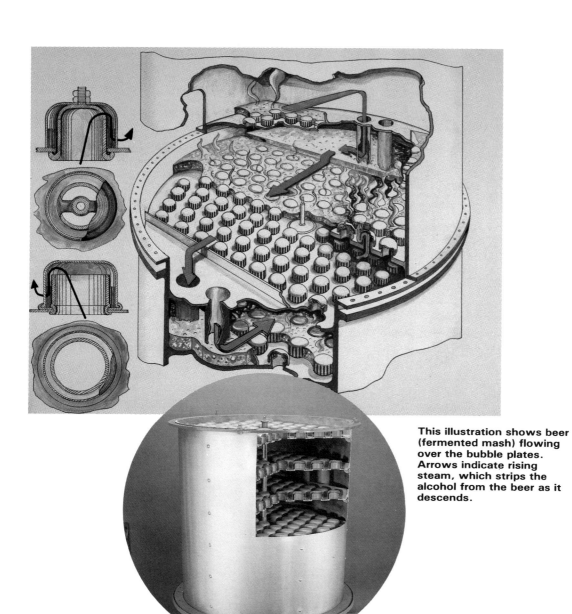

This illustration shows beer (fermented mash) flowing over the bubble plates. Arrows indicate rising steam, which strips the alcohol from the beer as it descends.

A cross-section through a column still, on display at The Seagram Museum

Distillation

After fermentation, the distiller separates the alcohol from the mash through primary distillation. In this process, the mash feeds into the top of the primary or beer still, which has been preheated with steam introduced at the bottom. The mash flows slowly down the column over a series of perforated plates. The perforations let the steam rise, but prevent the mash from flowing directly through the plates (see photo).

Alcohol boils at a lower temperature than water. As the mash heats up, the ascending steam strips the alcohol from the mash, leaving most of the water behind. The alcohol vapour moves to the top of the column, where a heat exchanger condenses the vapour into a liquid, which is then collected in a receiving tank. The remaining grain and water mixture, called whole stillage, flows to the bottom of the still, where machinery pumps it away for further processing into a livestock feed known as distillers' dried grains.

We now have whisky heavy in flavour, its character determined by the mash bill and by the distillation process itself. Its particular personality may be zesty, sweet, dry, fruity, soft, winey, or floral. If the distiller wants to use this once-distilled product as flavouring whisky, it can now be aged.

If the distiller desires a lighter, less flavourful base whisky, however, the distillate must undergo secondary distillation, or rectification. Secondary distillation removes many of the heavy flavouring components, or congeners. The final product will have a very light aroma and body.

For secondary distillation, the distiller can use the batch method or the continuous process method. In the batch method, the vapours from the heated whisky pass through a single distillation column. Since the various flavour components boil at different temperatures, these fractions separate out along the column. The low-boiling (more volatile) compounds — aldehydes and esters — come off first; the stillman collects these as "heads." The next part, known as the "centres" comes off next to become the base whisky. The final portion contains the higher boiling components (mostly fusel oils) and is removed as "tails." The stillman must use his nose along with instrument readings to determine when to make the heads-to-centres and centres-to-tails cuts.

When distillers produce their base whiskies in a continuous distillation unit, the heads, centres, and tails are separated out continuously in three or four separate columns.

The Origins of Distillation

Distillation is an ancient process. The word derives from the Latin word destillare, *meaning "to drop or trickle down." To put it simply, the vapours from a boiling liquid are collected, cooled, and then condensed back into a liquid. Distillation separates out the various components in a liquid by making use of the fact that the components vapourize, or evaporate, at different temperatures.*

The Romans distilled pine resin to make turpentine. Arabs used distillation to make essential oils for perfumes and flavourings. The first alcohol for beverage purposes was probably distilled by Italian monks in the twelfth century. Irish monks were the first to make whisky using this process. Today, many manufacturers use distillation for industrial processes such as refining crude oil and making drinking water from sea water.

Ageing: The Alchemy of Oak

By law, Canadian whisky must be aged for a minimum of three years in small wood barrels (of less than 680 litres, or 150 imperial gallons). Before going into the barrels, the new distillate undergoes quality control tests. The distiller adds just enough water so that it will mature at its optimum strength. Flavouring whiskies are matured at lower strengths than base whiskies.

As the new distillate ages in charred oak barrels, it transforms from a clear liquid with little character into a mellow-tasting, amber whisky. The marriage that takes place between wood and whisky smoothes out the harsh flavours of the raw distillate and introduces complex new flavour elements from the oak.

The barrels used in Canadian whisky are made of the heartwood of white oaks grown in the United States. New, charred, white oak barrels mature the heavy-bodied flavouring whiskies. Barrels used one or more times are then used to mature the lighter-bodied base whiskies. The presence of residual whisky flavours in the re-used barrels contributes to the distinctiveness of Canadian whisky.

The Seagram company sees its barrels as one of the most important factors in the development of the unique flavour of its finished whiskies. The company uses a complex system of

Pallet storage at Canadian Mist in Collingwood, Ontario. In most distilleries, rack storage of barrels has been replaced by pallet storage. Barrels are moved by machine rather than by hand.

barrels of various ages and histories. Each of its final, blended products has its own "barrel pedigree."

Whisky barrels "breathe" during maturation. In summer, the warm weather causes the pores of the oak to expand, or open, allowing whisky to enter. In winter, the pores contract, forcing the whisky out of the pores and back into the barrel. This whisky carries tannins and other flavouring elements from the wood into the maturing whisky. The charred wood also imparts a golden colour. With each annual "breath," known in the trade as "angel's breath," the whisky takes up more characteristics of the wood and more

Awakened from its long sleep, this Canadian whisky is ready to be bottled.

colour. Because whisky barrels breathe, the quality of the air around them influences the taste of the whisky. Distilleries in various parts of the country produce whiskies that reflect the conditions of temperature, humidity, and air quality in their particular area.

The amount of time that a whisky is aged depends on the type of whisky. Some reach optimum maturity in just three or four years. Others, especially the heavier flavouring whiskies, take at least five years. If left in the barrel too long, whisky can become woody and bitter. While the whiskies age, the blenders constantly evaluate them. At Seagram, for example, the blenders sample each type at least once a year, sending these samples to a blending library at the LaSalle Technical Centre in LaSalle, Quebec.

During the maturing process, up to 3 per cent of the barrel contents evaporate each year. This doesn't seem like a lot, but with a ten-year-old whisky, the final product will have shrunk by one-third. For this reason, excise officers must take losses due to evaporation into account.

Although distilleries are gigantic operations with computer controls for every aspect of the process, the final product must be evaluated and approved by the nose and palate of the master blender, whose task is to ensure that the products are of exactly the same high quality, year after year.

Blending: The Art of Whisky Making

Samuel Bronfman once said, "Distilling is a science, blending is an art." Even today, when distilleries are gigantic operations with computer controls for every aspect of the process, the final product must be evaluated and approved by a human nose and palate. Each company retains a master blender who must ensure that the products live up to the same high quality year after year. With highly developed sensory skills, the master blender and his or her associate blenders can distinguish among many subtly different whiskies. Because Canadian whiskies are created by blending several uniquely flavoured whiskies, the master blender's task is a complex one indeed.

Over one hundred and thirty years ago, Hiram Walker and Joseph E. Seagram developed two very different approaches to blending whisky.

The dumping room at Hiram Walker & Sons Limited. Walker blends its whiskies before ageing, while Seagram ages and then blends.

Today the two companies continue to follow the methods established by their founders, creating one of the most interesting questions in the Canadian whisky industry: should whisky be aged first and then blended, or blended and then aged?

At Hiram Walker, the blenders mix their base and flavouring whiskies together first, and then age the blended whisky. They believe that whisky manifests its true character-istics immediately after distillation. They blend their whiskies at that point, so that the constituents can "marry" during ageing.

At Seagram, the blenders age the base and flavouring whiskies separately, mixing them immediately before bottling. The Seagram approach is based on the belief that, before five or ten years of ageing, one cannot predict exactly what the final whisky will taste like. The type of barrel in which the whisky is stored can dramatically affect the final flavour. The very subtle changes of temperature and climate cannot be predicted. To maintain consistency in a product, they feel that blending separately aged whiskies is the right approach. Obviously, both distilleries must be right, since both produce excellent Canadian whiskies.

If whisky is blended after ageing, it is reduced to 40 per cent alcohol by volume by the addition of demineralized water, filtered, and allowed to rest and marry for up to seventy-two hours. Before bottling, sensory and instrument quality control tests ensure compliance with the standard. Unlike wine, whisky does not continue to mature or develop in the bottle.

Most of the old distilleries are gone now, or converted to other uses. But Canada's whisky heritage remains for us to enjoy. The Seagram Museum, an elegant building that incorporates an old barrel warehouse of the original Seagram company Waterloo plant, houses one of the world's best collections of artifacts and art relating to wines and spirits. In Walkerville, Hiram Walker gives regular tours of the distillery for visitors. The company plans to celebrate the centenary of the plant's renaissance office building, built in 1894, by turning it into a visitor centre to open in 1994.

The Gooderham and Worts complex, some thirty buildings on three-and-a-half acres just north of the Toronto waterfront, has been designated a National Historic Site by Parks Canada. The complex provides the best example of ninteenth-century industrial architecture in Canada, perhaps even in North America. In a 1988 paper, Parks Canada architectural historian Julie Harris wrote, "The Gooderham and Worts complex is a testimony to the economic importance of distilling in 19th century Canada, and to the development of a leading export product — Canadian whisky."[30]

Though the buildings have been vacant for a few years, the site is used frequently for television programs, films, and advertisments that require an authentic nineteenth-century setting. The owners, Allied-Lyons of Britain, have approval to develop the site for housing and commercial use, while maintaining its original character.

The Seagram Museum, which opened in 1984, has one of the world's most comprehensive collections of art and artifacts on wines and spirits.

Notes

1　Catherine Parr Traill,
The Backwoods of Canada,
letter 9, April 18, 1833 (London:
Charles Knight, 1836), 135.

2　The Sydenham Township
Council and the Women's
Institutes of Sydenham
Township,
*The History of Sydenham
Township* (Sydenham: 1967),
739.

3　Helen Schmid and Sid
Rutherford,
*Out of the Mists: A History of
Clarke Township* (Orono,
Ontario: Helen Schmid, 1975),
140.

4　Colonel Sam B. Steele,
Forty Years in Canada (Toronto:
McClelland, Goodchild &
Stewart Limited, 1915), 54.

5　John McTaggart,
Three Years in Canada (London:
H. Colburn, 1829). John
McTaggart was chief engineer for
the Rideau Canal.

6　E.B Shuttleworth,
The Windmill and Its Times
(Toronto: Edward D. Apted,
Printer, 1924), 71-2.

7　John Graves Simcoe,
Letter to Henry Dundas, August
2, 1704, in *Simcoe Papers*, vol.
3, 1794-1795 (Ontario Historical
Society), 3.

8　Merrill Denison,
The Barley and the Stream,
(Toronto: McClelland and
Stewart Limited, 1955), 120.

9　*Montreal Gazette*,
As quoted in "William
Gooderham," in *The Canadian
Biographical Dictionary and
Portrait Gallery of Eminent and
Self-Made Men*, Ontario volume
(Toronto: American Biographical
Publishing Company, 1880), 66.

10　*The Leeds and Grenville,
Lanark, and Renfrew County
Directory* (1859).

11　*The Conservative Messenger*,
Prescott (1862).

12　Francis Chauvin,
"Hiram Walker and the
Development of the Walker
Institutions in Walkerville,
Ontario," unpublished (1956),
ch. 14, p. 9.

13　Ibid.,
as quoted in the *Detroit News*,
ch. 29, p. 5-6.

14　E. B. Shuttleworth,
The Windmill, 68.

15　Thomas Molson,
personal diary, May 26, 1836, as
quoted in Merrill Denison, *The
Barley and the Stream* (Toronto:
McClelland and Stewart Limited,
1955), 170.

16　Francis Chauvin,
"Hiram Walker," ch. 9, p. 3.

17　Michael Jackson,
The World Guide to Whisky
(London: Dorling Kindersley
Limited, 1987), 128.

18　Francis Chauvin,
"Hiram Walker," ch. 33, p. 7.

19　Graeme Decarie,
"My Country, Wet or Dry," in
Horizon Canada (Quebec City:
Centre for the Study of Teaching
in Canada, 1987), 134.

20　Dr. William "Tiger" Dunlop,
*Statistical Sketches of Upper
Canada for the Use of
Emigrants: By a Backwoodsman*
(London: John Murray, 1832),
mispaged.

21　Colonel Thomas Talbot,
as quoted in Fred Coyne Hamil,
*Lake Erie Baron: The Story of
Colonel Thomas Talbot*
(Toronto: Macmillan Co. of
Canada, 1955), 229.

22　Stephen Leacock,
as quoted in Gerald A. Hallowell,
*Prohibition in Ontario, 1919–
1923*, research publication no. 2
(Ontario Historical Society,
1972), 85.

23　Father Charles Chiniquy,
"Manual of the Temperance
Society, Dedicated to the Youth
of Canada," pamphlet (1847),
Archives of Ontario, no. 17.

24　Nellie Mooney McClung,
as quoted in Mary Hallett and
Marilyn Davis, *Firing the
Heather: The Life and Times of
Nellie Mooney McClung*,
(Saskatoon: Fifth House
Publishing, 1993), 81.

25　Ernest Drury,
"Temperance: The Vital Issue,"
pamphlet (Toronto: 1923),
Archives of Ontario, no. 29.

26　Egerton Ryerson,
Christian Monitor (July 2, 1835).

27　Stephen Leacock,
As quoted in Peter C. Newman,
*Bronfman Dynasty–The
Rothschilds of the New World*
(Toronto: McClelland and
Stewart, 1978), 79.

28　Anon.
American prohibition song, in
the Duke of Windsor, *A King's
Story*, (1951); variant in B.
Riddell, *Regional Disparity*
(1972), 5.

29　Peter Melrose,
personal communication with
the author, February 16, 1994.

30　Julie Harris,
"The Gooderham and Worts
Distillery Complex, 2 Trinity
Street, Toronto, Ontario,"
agenda paper 1988-38 (Ottawa:
Historical Sites and Monuments
Board of Canada, November
1988), 361.

200 **B**ibliography

The author found several books particularly useful and interesting. These are marked with asterisks. The reader may want to consult them for further information.

CHAPTER 1

Brown, Howard Morton.
Lanark Legacy: 19th Century Glimpses of an Ontario County. Perth: The Corporation of the County of Lanark, 1984.
Garland, M.A., and J. Talmon. *
"Pioneer Drinking Habits and the Rise of Temperance Agitation in Upper Canada Prior to 1840," 1924. In F.H. Armstrong, H.A. Stevenson, and J.D. Wilson, eds., *Aspects of Nineteenth Century Ontario*, Toronto: University of Toronto Press, 1974.
Grey, James.
Booze. Toronto: Macmillan of Canada, 1972.
Lender, Mark, and James Kirby Martin.
Drinking in America. New York: The Free Press, 1982.
McBurney, Margaret, and Mary Byers.
Tavern in the Town. Toronto: University of Toronto Press, 1987.
Rannie, William F. *
Canadian Whisky: The Product and the Industry. Lincoln: W.F. Rannie, Publisher, 1976.
Rorabaugh, David.
The Alcoholic Republic. Oxford: Oxford University Press, 1979.
Schmid, Helen, and Sid Rutherford.
Out of the Mists: A History of Clarke Township. Orono, Ontario: Helen Schmid, 1975.
Steele, Colonel Sam B.
Forty Years in Canada. Toronto: McClelland, Goodchild & Stewart Limited, 1915.
Warsh, Cheryl Krasnick, ed.
Drink in Canada. Montreal: McGill-Queen's University Press, 1993.

CHAPTER 2

Denison, Merrill. *
The Barley and the Stream: The Molson Story. Toronto: McClelland and Stewart, 1955.

Harris, Julie.
"The Gooderham and Worts Distillery Complex, 2 Trinity Street, Toronto, Ontario." Agenda Paper 1988-38. Ottawa: Historical Sites and Monuments Board of Canada, November 1988.
Newell, Dianne, and Ralph Greenhill.
Survivals: Aspects of Industrial Archaeology in Ontario. Boston: Boston Mills Press, 1989.
Shuttleworth, E.B. *
The Windmill and Its Times. Toronto: Edward D. Apted, Printer, 1924.

CHAPTER 3

Chauvin, Francis X. *
"Hiram Walker and the Development of the Walker Institutions in Walkerville, Ontario." Master's thesis, 1927.
Mika, Nick, and Helma Mika.
Belleville: The Good Old Days. Belleville, Ontario: Mika Publishing Company, 1975.
Teatero, William.
"Notes on the History of Wiser's Distillery Limited." Undergraduate thesis, Queen's University, 1977.

CHAPTER 4

Canadian Illustrated News. *
April 25, 1863. National Archives of Canada.
Denison, Merrill. *
The Barley and the Stream.
Lafayette Byrn, M.
The Complete Practical Distiller. Philadelphia: Henry C. Baird, 1853.
Shuttleworth, E.B. *
The Windmill.
Tomlinson, Charles.
The Illustration of Trades. ca. 1860. (Can be seen at Upper Canada Village.)

CHAPTER 5

Cook, Sharon Anne.
"Letitia Youmans: Ontario's Nineteenth-Century Temperance Educator." *Ontario History* 74, 4 (December 1992): 329–42.
Decarie, Graeme.
Prohibition in Canada. Vol 29 of *Canada's Visual History*. National Museums of Canada.
Decarie, Graeme.
"The Prohibition Movement in Ontario: 1819–1916." Ph.D. Thesis, Queen's University, 1972.
Garland, M.A., and J. Talmon. *
"Pioneer Drinking Habits."

Tennyson, Brian Douglas.
"Sir William Hearst and the Ontario Temperance Act." *Ontario History* 55, 4 (1963).
Youmans, Letitia.
Campaign Echoes. Toronto: William Briggs, 1893.

CHAPTER 6

Andrieux, Jean-Pierre.
Over the Side. Lincoln: W.F. Rannie, 1984.
Andrieux, Jean-Pierre. *
Probibition and St. Pierre. Lincoln: W.F. Rannie, 1983.
Gervais, Martin. *
The Rumrunners. Willowdale, Ontario: Firefly Press, 1980.
Hennigar, Ted R.
The Rum Running Years. Hantsport, Nova Scotia: Lancelot Press, 1981.
Miles, Fraser.
Slow Boat on Rum Row. Madeira Park, British Columbia: Harbour Publications, 1992.
Parker, Marion, and Robert Tyrrell.
Rum-Runner: The Life and Times of Johnny Schnarr. Victoria, British Columbia: Orca Books, 1988.

CHAPTER 7

History of the House of Seagram.
Seagram Papers, Seagram Museum Archives.
Rannie, William F.
Canadian Whisky.
Rannie, William F.
"Old, Big, Colourful: The Distilling Industry." *Canadian Geographical Journal* 93, 3 (1976): 20–27.

CHAPTER 8

Association of Canadian Distillers.
1992 Annual Report.

CHAPTER 9

Delavante, Michael P.
"Spirits in the Making." Unpublished. 1987.
Jackson, Michael.
The World Book of Whisky. Toronto: Prentice-Hall Canada Inc., 1987.
Liquor Control Board of Ontario. *
"Canadian Whisky Product Knowledge." Seminar presented by A.G. Dawe of Joseph E. Seagram & Sons, Limited, on May 4, 1993.
Murphy, Brian.
The World Book of Whisky. Rand McNally & Company, 1979.

# Index

２００ Picture and Illustration Credits

Alberta Distillers Limited: 126; 132 top; 141

Alberta Wheat Pool: 118; 129

Archives of Ontario: 79, S 15001

Association of Canadian Distillers: 123 both; 123; 126

Canada Malting Company: 130; 131

Canadian Mist Distillers Limited: 112; 140

Chapman and Hall Limited: 50, as reproduced from Karl M. Herstein and Thomas C. Gregory, *Chemistry and Technology of Wines and Liquor* (London: 1935), p. 89

City of Toronto Archives: 17 bottom, A 85-31; 18 top, SC 583-86; 18 bottom, SC 583-6; 20, SC 583-98; 53, SC 583-87; 54, SC 583-18

Corby Distilleries Limited: 22

Department of Customs & Excise: 89; 92 bottom

Glenbow–Alberta Institute; 3, NA-1751-5; 4 bottom, NC-2-383; 6 top, NA-550-18; 6 bottom, NA-967-1; 9 top, 782-2; 61 top, NA-3199-1; 63 bottom, NA-1639-1; 78, NA-3229-20; 82 top, NC-6-4040

Hastings County Historical Society Archives: 36 top, HC1522; 36 bottom, HC1528

Hiram Walker & Sons Ltd.: xii; 31; 32; 34 all; 40 top; 41; 106; 107; 108; 109 both; 120; 121 both; 124; 135; 136; 143

Hotel Robert Museum: 96 both top

Houghton Mifflin Company: 83, as reproduced from Alastair Moray, *The Diary of a Rum-runner* (Houghton Mifflin, 1929)

The Huron County Museum Collection, Goderich: 68 top left

The Imperial Oil Collection: ix, C.W. Jefferys

Kingston Public Library: 75

Knickles Studio, Lunenburg, Nova Scotia: 94

Leeds & Grenville County Archives: 25; 26 both

Liquor Control Board of Ontario: 77

McCord Museum of Canadian History–Notman Photographic Archives: 15 top, 1332 View; 21 top, 30178-I

Metropolitan Toronto Reference Library: 4 top, B2-6, Repro. T11069

Metropolitan Toronto Reference Library and York University: 81 top

The Molson Companies: 13; 15 bottom, as reproduced in Merrill Denison, *The Barley and the Stream: The Molson Story* (Toronto: McClelland and Stewart, 1955)

The Moncton Museum: 72

National Archives of Canada: 8, PA120150; 11 top, C130539; 12 left, C8111; 18 centre, C134285; 19, C134288; 24, PA33859; 30, PA134862; 33 top, PA31249; 33 bottom, PA30531; 35, PA28708; 51, C134290, *Canadian Illustrated News*; 52 top, C134289, *CIN*; 52 bottom, C134291, *CIN*; 59, NC134286, *CIN*; 61 right, C62795; 62 top, C140769; 62 bottom, PA87397; 63 top, C5084; 66 top, C55095; 68 bottom left, C122927; 68 right, C7869; 69 left, C140676; 69 right, PA30212; 70 left, C14235; 70 right, PA110157; 73 top, PA72521; 73 bottom, PA72520

National Archives of Canada, Molson Archives: 14, C141192, MG 28 111 57 vol. 34

National Library of Canada: 71, NL 18358

Perth Courier: 39 top

The Perth Museum: 37; 38

Photo Studio Y. Andrieux/Hotel Robert Museum: 92 top; 95; 96 bottom

Provincial Archives of Manitoba: 9 left, N371; 10

Provincial Archives of Manitoba, Hudson's Bay Company Archives: 5, N7688; 76, N7687

Provincial Archives of New Brunswick: 66 left, P5368

The Royal Ontario Museum: 11 bottom, 951-158-17

Saskatchewan Archives Board: 2 bottom, A2270; 82 bottom, A7536

The Seagram Museum: x; xi; 2 top; 4 centre; 7; 12 bottom right; 12 top right; 16 top, E.B. Shuttleworth, *The Windmill and Its Times* (Toronto: Edward D. Apted, Printer, 1924); 17 top, *The Windmill*; 16 bottom; 21 bottom; 27, 1900.06; 28, 1900.07C; 29 top, 1800.01; 29 bottom; 39 bottom, 1925.06; 40 bottom; 42 top, ARC 86.5.6; 42 bottom right and left; 43; 44 both; 46; 47; 48; 49, *The Windmill*; 56 all; 57 both, *The Seagram Museum*; 58; 64; 65, George Cruikshank, *The Bottle and the Drunkard's Children*, (New York: Frederick A. Stokes, Printer); 74; 80; 81 bottom; 93; 97; 98; 99; 100; 101; 102; 103; 104 both; 113; 122; 125; 127; 132 bottom; 133; 134; 138 top, ARC 82.3.8; 138 bottom; 142; 144

Toronto Sun: 67 bottom, February 27, 1977 (as reproduced from original produced by an Ontario Temperance Society, 1915)

E.A. Turner: 23, as reproduced from Thad. W.H. Leavitt, *History of Leeds and Grenville Ontario, From 1749 to 1879* (Brockville: Recorder Press, 1879).

Upper Canada Village: 1

Windsor Star: 84 all; 85; 86; 90; 91